Comfort Food

Vegan Cooking with Over 60 Gluten Free Recipes

Jeanne K. Horning

OlivePress
צהר זית

Messianic & Christian Publisher

Published by
Olive Press צהר זית
Messianic and Christian Publisher

www.olivepresspublisher.com

Messianic & Christian Publisher

Our prayer at Olive Press is that we may help make the Word of Adonai fully known, that it spread rapidly and be glorified everywhere. We hope our books help open people's eyes so they will turn from darkness to Light and from the power of the adversary to God and to trust in ישוע Yeshua (Jesus). (From II Thess. 3:1; Col. 1:25; Acts 26:18,15 NRSV and CJB, the *Complete Jewish Bible*) For this book, our prayer is that people eat healthy so they can be healed and have energy to do the Kingdom work God is calling them to do.

Cover and interior photos © 2013 by the author
Cover design by the author
Author photo by Andrea Hubbard
Interior design by Olive Press

Comfort Food: Vegan Cooking with Over 60 Gluten Free Recipes

ISBN 978-0-9855241-7-3
Printed in the USA.

1. Cooking: Vegan 2. Cooking: Health and Healing: Gluten Free

Genesis 1:29

Then God said, "I give you every seed bearing plant on the face of the earth and every tree that has fruit with seed in it. They will be yours for food" (NIV).

Acknowledgements

A very grateful thank you to my Lord and savior, Jesus Christ, and the Holy Spirit for the nudges to write this book as well as His love, grace, and encouragement in all things.

Also, a warm, fuzzy thank you to my family and friends for loaning me their taste buds countless times. The words "try this please" and "please let me know if you like A, B, or C better" are phrases they came to know very well. Their enthusiasm and feedback were invaluable!

Thank you also for giving these recipes a try! My prayer is that you will enjoy preparing as well as eating the food you find in these pages.

Joyous Blessings from my kitchen to yours!   -Jeanne

Table of Contents

Recipes

Recipes (Continued)

Abbreviations

"	-	inch/inches
'	-	foot/feet
#	-	pound(s)
%	-	percent
&	-	and
approx	-	approximately
cont	-	continued
med	-	medium
oz	-	ounce
P.B.	-	Peanut Butter
pkg	-	package
S.S.	-	Sweet and Spicy
tsp	-	teaspoon
T	-	tablespoon
temp	-	temperature
x	-	by
xv	-	extra virgin
xvoo	-	extra virgin olive oil
xvco	-	extra virgin coconut oil

Instructions Included...

In this book you will find the ingredients in the order to be used, followed by very detailed, easy-to-follow instructions to answer your questions and make your food preparation more enjoyable. Gluten Free recipe titles are marked with two asterisks (**); recipes with a Gluten Free option are marked with one asterisk (*). The list of "Tips" at the end of this book on page 162 are also well worth reading. If you have any questions you are welcome to e-mail me at:

stonehillbakerycooking@gmail.com

Coriander Lentil Soup

Creamy Potato Veggie Soup

Soups

Miso Veggie Soup

Chunky Corn Chowder

For those first cool nights when there is fresh corn still available, this is especially good!

10 cups water
2 cups white or yellow onions, chopped fine
2 cups celery, chopped
10 cups potatoes, diced
2 large cloves garlic, chopped fine (approx 2 T)

8 cups fresh sweet corn cut off the cob (5 or 6 large ears)
1 T whole salt
½ tsp fresh ground black pepper

6-7 T Italian parsley, chopped fine

Cream sauce:
1 cup xv olive oil
2 T lecithin, granular (or liquid)
1 cup spelt flour
1 ½ tsp whole salt
4 cups plain soy milk

For the cream sauce, heat the oil over medium heat in a thick-bottomed pan.
Add the lecithin and stir for a minute.
Add the flour and salt, stirring constantly until bubbles.
Continue stirring while you slowly pour the soy milk in. Stir until it begins to simmer.
Remove from heat and set aside.
In a large stock pot with a heavy bottom, bring the water to a boil.
Add the onions, garlic, celery and potato. Simmer until half cooked.
Stir in the corn and simmer until the veggies are crisp-tender (tender but slightly crisp, see p. 170).
Mix in the cream sauce and parsley. Bring back to a simmer.

Serve hot with whole grain bread and a lettuce salad for a happy tummy!

Options:
- Using frozen corn for this is very good too.
- If you would like a thicker soup, shake together 2 T arrowroot powder and 3 T water and add to the simmering soup. Stir constantly until bubbles. Repeat the process if you prefer a thicker soup still.

Coriander Lentil Soup**

Even those who aren't big soup fans love this one!

2 ½ T xv olive oil
2 medium onions, chopped (1-1 ¼ cups)
2 large cloves garlic, chopped fine (2 T)
1 tsp coriander
1 tsp cumin
1 tsp turmeric
1 large carrot, diced (1 cup)

3 stalks celery, diced (1 ½ cups)

4 cups fresh or canned tomatoes, coarsely chopped
8 cups water
4 cubes veggie bouillon
3 cups red lentils
1 tsp basil
1 tsp cinnamon
¼ tsp cayenne pepper
2 T fresh parsley, chopped fine

Sauté first 7 ingredients on low, adding in order listed. Stir constantly until half cooked.
Stir in remaining ingredients, excluding parsley. Bring to a boil.
Reduce heat to a low simmer, cover and cook for 1-1 ½ hours, stirring occasionally until lentils are soft and veggies tender.
Stir in parsley and adjust seasonings.

For a large crowd, double the recipe.

Option: Replace red lentils with brown or green lentils. Just as good, but quite a difference in taste!

Creamy Broccoli Soup**

This soup is so quick, so delicious, and surprisingly filling!

½ cup water
½ T xv olive oil
1-2 cups small (¾") broccoli flowerettes

3 T xv olive oil
½ cup well packed fresh basil
4 cups plain soy milk
4 cups water
3 veggie bouillon cubes
8 cups broccoli flowerettes
⅓ cup tahini
1 T Braggs liquid aminos
3 T arrowroot powder shaken up with ¼ cup water

Heat a small fry pan on low.
Add the approx ½ cup water, ½ T xv olive oil, and the 1-2 cups small broccoli flowerettes.
Cover and simmer gently 1-2 minutes until crisp-tender (see p. 170). Set aside uncovered.
Heat oil in a very large heavy bottomed stock pot on low.
Add basil and stir 1 minute.
Slowly stir in 3 cups soy milk then water and broken up bouillon cubes.
Bring to a simmer (watching carefully as it may bubble up) and stir in broccoli.
Reduce heat to just a simmer when covered and cook until crisp-tender (2-4 minutes).
Place 1 cup soy milk and ⅓ cup tahini in Vitamix blender and mix well.
Add a couple cups of broccoli/liquid mix to it and blend on high until smooth.
Pour this into a second large pot and blend the rest, 3 cups at a time.
Mix in the Braggs.
Bring soup back to a simmer, pour the arrowroot/water mix in and stir until just comes back to a
    boil and thickens.
Remove from the heat, stir in the flowerettes and serve.

Options:

- For the serious basil fans, up to 1 cup basil can be used.
- If you know anyone who has let their broccoli go to flower, the parts that snap off easily can still be used for this soup.

Creamy Cauliflower Soup*

This will fill you up and warm you down to your toes.

4 cups potatoes, diced
4 cups cauliflower flowerettes
2 cups carrots, sliced thick
5 large cloves garlic, coarsely chopped (5 T)
4 tsp whole salt
8 cups water
2 large stalks celery, sliced thick
2 ¼ cups cooking onions, chopped coarse

3 cups lightly steamed cauliflower flowerettes

Cream Sauce
6 T xv olive oil
6 T kamut flour
½ tsp Dijon mustard
3 cups plain soy milk
¼ cup tahini
3-4 T fresh dill, chopped fine (1 ½ -2 T dry)
2-3 T Italian parsley, chopped fine

Simmer all in the water down to onions & cook until veggies are crisp-tender. (Do not overcook!)
Blend in the Vitamix blender until creamy.

While the veggies are cooking make the cream sauce.
Heat the oil on medium low. Stir in the flour and mustard until bubbles.
Gradually add the milk stirring constantly on medium heat until just comes to a boil.
Whisk in tahini, dill, and parsley.
Add to soup, stir in steamed flowerettes.
Adjust the amount of dill and parsley to taste.
Serve hot.

Gluten Free Option: Omit 6 T kamut flour. When soup is completed and back to a simmer, shake together ¼ cup arrowroot powder with ⅓ cup water. Stir into soup until it bubbles. Remove from the heat. For thicker soup, add an additional 1 T arrowroot/1 T water mixture bringing back to a simmer with each addition.

Creamy Potato Veggie Soup*

Potato soup is a perennial comfort food.
With a variety of veggies included, it is a hearty meal all by itself.

2 ½-3 quarts water
2 medium onions, chopped (2 cups)
3-4 cloves garlic, chopped fine (3-4 T)
1 T whole salt
12 cups white potatoes, chopped fine
¼ cup flat leaf parsley, chopped fine

Cream Sauce
½ cup xv olive oil
2 cups onion, chopped
¼ cup granular lecithin
2 bay leaves
1 tsp whole salt
¼- ½ tsp black pepper
4 cups green cabbage, cut in ½-1" square pieces
1 cup carrots, chopped
2 ½-3 cups celery, chopped
2 large cloves garlic, chopped fine (2 T)
⅓ cup spelt flour
6 cups plain soy milk

In a very large stock pot, bring the first 4 ingredients to a boil.
Add potatoes, return to a boil and gently simmer until potatoes are just tender but not soft.
Blend ⅔ of mixture in a blender until smooth and return to pot.

Cream Sauce:
Gently sauté first 10 ingredients until veggies are crisp-tender (see p. 170).
Stir in flour then slowly stir in soy milk. Stir constantly until thickens.
Add to the potatoes and stir in the parsley. Adjust seasonings if needed and serve.

It is filling on its own, but add a green salad and whole grain bread, if you like, and enjoy!
This soup is even better the second day, as most soups are.
Why so much soup? It's nice to freeze some for future meals. (It will thin out a bit when thawed but is still delicious.)
Gluten Free Option: Omit spelt flour. When the completed soup has come back to a simmer, shake together ¼ cup arrowroot powder with ⅓ cup water. Stir into the soup and continue stirring until it comes back to a simmer and serve.

Gazpacho**

Cool and refreshing on a hot summer evening.

Dressing:
2 T red wine vinegar
2 T xv olive oil
⅛ tsp whole salt (optional)
1 clove garlic, minced (1T)

3 cups fresh ripe tomatoes
1 cucumber, seeded or burpless
½ cup green pepper
3-4 T fresh parsley, chopped fine
⅓ cup red or white sweet onion, chopped fine

Whisk together salad dressing and set aside.
Dice veggies to ¼"-⅓".
Blend together all ingredients, then stir in the dressing.
Leave out 30-40 minutes stirring occasionally.
Cover and refrigerate.

Option: replace red wine vinegar with apple cider vinegar.
Option: Blend at varying degrees for either salad, side dish, or soup.

H. S. Black Bean Soup**

One pot, one hour, until a warm full tummy!

¼ cup xv olive oil
½ cup onion, chopped
1 medium clove garlic, minced (½ T)
1 tsp cumin
¼ tsp coriander
4 cups drained black beans
4 cups canned tomatoes, chopped up a bit
½ tsp oregano
½ cup sweet red pepper, diced
½ cup green pepper, diced
½ tsp whole salt
¼ tsp black pepper
½ tsp honey

Gently sauté the first 5 ingredients until onion is half cooked.
Stir in the remaining ingredients in the order listed.
Bring to a boil and simmer on low for 50-60 minutes, stirring occasionally.
Serve.

Hot/Cold Tomato Soup**

A nice quick soup, and a good way to use up extra tomatoes.

Just blend enough raw tomatoes in Vitamix to get 4 cups, then proceed as shown below.

4 cups tomato puree
⅓ cup white sweet onion, chopped
1 T fresh Italian parsley, chopped
¾ tsp honey
¼ tsp fresh ground black pepper
¼ tsp whole salt
1 veggie bouillon cube
1 large clove garlic, or a 6" long piece of garlic scape, chopped
2 T xv olive oil
¼ cup plain soy milk (optional)

Place all in a Vitamix blender and run on high a couple minutes until very smooth.
Chill, or eat as is.

Option: Put all in a pot and simmer on low until onion is soft. Serve immediately.

Lentil Soup & Greens**

This is a very filling, satisfying soup, especially on a cool night.

2-3 T xv olive oil
1 large onion, chopped (1 ½ cup)
1 large clove garlic (1 T)
2 carrots, diced (1 ½ cups)
3 large stalks celery (2 cups)

1 ¼ cups brown or green lentils
¼ cup red lentils
1 quart canned tomatoes and juice
6 cups water
¼ tsp black pepper (optional)
2 tsp whole salt
¾ # escarole, rinsed and chopped in 1 ½" squares. (approx half a large bunch)

Sauté the first 5 ingredients in a large soup pot on low until veggies are half cooked.
Stir in the next 6 ingredients, bring to a low simmer and cook covered until the lentils are just soft.
Stir in the escarole. Simmer until escarole is soft.

This is especially good with a salad and fresh bread.

Options:
- Add a tablespoon of fresh lemon juice at the end.
- Replace the escarole with yellow ribbed swiss chard including the ribs, or chinese cabbage, or spinach.
- A little chopped fresh basil added the last few minutes is a nice change, too.

Minestrone Soup**

This is truly a meal in a bowl. A salad and fresh whole grain bread is still nice company though.

6 T xv olive oil
2 ½ cups yellow cooking onions, chopped (2 large)
5-6 large cloves garlic, chopped fine (5-6 T)
2 ½ cups celery, diced (3 large stalks)
2-3 carrots, diced (2 cups)

4 quarts canned tomatoes (128 oz)
¾ cup corn kernels
¾ cup fresh green beans, cut in ½" pieces
¼ cup packed fresh basil, chopped fine (4 tsp dried)
3-4 tsp fresh oregano, chopped fine (1 tsp dried)
1 cup chickpeas, semi drained
2 cups black beans, semi drained
1 cup pinto beans, semi drained
1 ½ cups cooked whole barley
1 tsp fresh ground black pepper
1 T plus ½ tsp whole salt
2 large bay leaves
1 tsp dry rosemary, chopped fine (2 T fresh)
1 tsp honey

¼-½ cup fresh Italian parsley, chopped fine

Gently sauté the onion, garlic, celery, and carrots in the olive oil for 2 or 3 minutes, stirring occasionally.
Cut the tomatoes into smaller pieces. (Slicing a few times right in the jar or can is all that's needed.)
Stir in the tomatoes along with everything else but the parsley.
Bring to a boil, reduce heat to a low simmer while covered and cook 1½ - 2 hours stirring every 30 minutes. When the veggies are just done and the tomatoes have mostly liquefied, test and adjust seasonings accordingly. Stir in the parsley and enjoy.

Options:

- Although it's always good to go by the recipe at first for a baseline, this recipe is very flexible.
- Don't have chickpeas? Put in more pinto or black beans.
- No corn, green beans, or even parsley on hand? Leave them out.
- Like a thinner soup? Add more tomatoes and a bit more olive oil.
- Really like fresh basil? Use up to twice as much.
- Like a more savory soup? Add 2 more tablespoons oil.
- Should you find yourself with too many fresh tomatoes in the fall, peel and chop 4 quarts or blend 4 quarts worth of tomatoes in your blender to replace the canned tomatoes. Mmm...
- Want to add whole barley? Bring to a simmer 3 cups water and ½ cup whole barley. Cover and cook on a low simmer 1-1 ½ hours until soft and fully cooked. (How old the barley is will have an effect on how long it takes to cook.) If there is some water left when fully cooked, just toss into the soup with the barley.

Miso Veggie Soup**

This is a great soup when you have a cold... or when you're just cold!

2 cups baby portabella mushrooms, sliced thin (⅛")
1 cup carrots, sliced thin
1 cup green cabbage, sliced thin and cut in 1" lengths
1 cup celery, sliced thin
½ cup onion, sliced thin
2 large cloves garlic, chopped fine (2 T)
1 -1 ½ tsp fresh ginger, finely grated
2 T xv olive oil
½ cup green pepper, sliced thin (optional)
6 cups water
3-4 T red miso
2 scallions, sliced thin (optional)

Gently sauté first 6 ingredients in oil for a minute.
Stir in green peppers, ginger, and water.
Heat to a low simmer and cook until veggies are crisp-tender (see p. 170).
Remove from heat and stir in the miso.
A sprinkling of scallions in each bowl before serving is an attractive as well as tasty addition.
(You may need to add 1 or 2 cups water to thin toward the end of cooking.)

One Pot Lentil Soup**

For real lentil lovers. This is the quickest, simplest soup to make.

¼ cup xv coconut oil
1 large bay leaf
1 medium onion (⅔ cup)
1 clove garlic, chopped fine (1T)
1 medium carrot, diced (⅔ cup)
2 large stalks celery, diced (1 ⅓ cups)

¼ tsp black pepper
2 tsp salt
2 ½ cups brown or green lentils
¼ cup red lentils
½ tsp liquid lecithin
10 cups water
2 cups diced potatoes

1 T chopped fresh parsley (optional)
1 tsp fresh lemon juice (optional)

Set parsley and lemon juice aside.

Then there are three choices:

1. Sauté the first 6 ingredients together until half cooked then add the rest, which affords you a little more flavor in the veggies.

2. Toss it all in the pot at once, bring to a low simmer (bubbling, but little bubbles) and cook covered for approx 1 ½ -2 ½ hours until lentils are nice and soft.
Stir every 30-40 minutes if possible; if not, it'll survive.

3. Warm coconut oil until it liquifies. Mix all ingredients well in a crock pot, cover as always and cook on low for 6-8 hours until lentils are soft.
Stir every 2 hours, if possible, for mixture to cook more evenly,.
When soup is done, stir in parsley and/or lemon juice, if you like.

This is my idea of fast food: to eat today and the rest of the week. It freezes well, too.

S. S. Squash Soup**

Spicy or sweet, this is a warm, satisfying soup with staying power.
Can't decide which to make? Split the finished base in two, cut the spice amount of each in half and try both!

Base:
6 cups water
1 ½ tsp whole salt
4 ½ cups raw butternut squash in ¾" cubes, unskinned (approx 1 ½ #)
1 cup carrots, diced small
1 cup red lentils

¼ cup light olive oil
2 tsp honey

Spicy mix
1 tsp ginger
2 tsp curry powder

Sweet mix
1 tsp cinnamon
¼ tsp clove
⅛ tsp nutmeg

Place first 6 ingredients in a large pot.
Bring to boil, then reduce to a low simmer when covered.
Cook until lentils and veggies are soft, about 30-40 minutes.
Place 2-3 cups at a time in a large food processor and process until smooth.
Return to pot. Stir in one of the spice mixes.
Let the flavors meld for 10-15 minutes and serve.

Options: For a lighter flavored version of the spicy mix, add ¼ - ½ cup creamed coconut milk.

Simple Black Bean Soup**

3 T xv olive oil
1 large onion, chopped (1 cup)
2-3 large cloves garlic, chopped fine
⅔ cup celery, chopped fine
1 tsp whole salt
1 tsp cumin
½ T chili powder
½ tsp black pepper
4-5 cups black beans, drained
1 cup sweet red pepper, diced
1 ½ cups bean juice
½ tsp honey
2 cups tomato puree or canned tomatoes

Lightly sauté the first 4 ingredients until half cooked, stirring frequently.
Add the next 4 ingredients for a minute or so stirring constantly, then add remaining ingredients.
Simmer for 1-2 hrs until veggies are soft and soup is desired consistency.

Serve with whole grain bread and a salad, and you have dinner!

Options:

- To thicken the soup a little quicker: Toward the end, shake up 1 T arrowroot powder with 2 T water and stir into soup. Stir constantly until returns to a simmer.

- If you're in a hurry, toss it all in a pot and simmer until done.

- Cook it in a crock pot on low for 6-8 hours. (Stirring every hour or so if possible will help the soup cook more evenly.)

Split Pea & Lentil Soup**

Plain split pea soup is good; adding in red lentils and a few spices, is even better.

¼ cup xv olive oil
3-4 T garlic, chopped fine
1 ½ cups onion, chopped
1 tsp cumin
2 tsp coriander

2 cups celery, chopped
1 ½ cups carrots, chopped
3 ½-4 tsp whole salt
½-¾ tsp black pepper
3 cups green split peas
1 cup red lentils
14-15 cups water
4 cups white potatoes, diced
¼-⅓ cup fresh Italian parsley

In a large pot sauté onion, garlic, and spices in oil on low for 1-2 minutes.
Stir in the carrots, celery, salt and pepper. Sauté, stirring frequently for another couple minutes.
Add in the water, raise temperature and bring to a boil.
Stir in the potatoes, bring back to a low simmer, cover and cook for approx an hour until legumes
   are soft and veggies are tender.
Stir in the parsley.

Set out the whole grain bread and a salad, and dinner is served!

Option:
- Mix all but the parsley together & bring to a simmer. Not quite the same as above, but very good.
- Cook in a crock pot approx 3-4 hrs on high; 7-8 hrs on low. (Stir every couple hours if possible.)

Thanksgiving Soup**

All those fall herbs in a hot satisfying soup!

4 cups hot water
1 ½ cubes veggie bouillon
1T xv olive oil
½- ¾ cup celery, diced (1 large stalk)
½ cup carrots, diced (1 medium)
½ cup onion, chopped fine (½ large yellow)
2 tsp garlic, chopped fine
¾ tsp whole salt
½ tsp black or white pepper

½ tsp thyme
½ tsp rosemary, broken into small pieces
¼ tsp poultry seasoning
1 small bay leaf
5 cups cooked navy pea beans (or great northern)
1T tomato paste
½ cup whole barley
1/16 tsp cayenne pepper

1T fresh parsley, chopped fine

Mix all but the parsley into a crockpot. Cover and cook: 5-7 hours on high, or 8-10 hours on low, until all ingredients are fully cooked. Mix in parsley and serve.

Options:

- Replace barley with quinoa.

- Increase hot water to 8-10 cups and replace 5 cups cooked beans with 2 cups dry beans.

- If you'd like the soup thicker when it has finished cooking, shake up 2T water with 1T arrowroot powder and stir in until it returns to a simmer; repeat if desired.

- Replace white beans with either black beans or brown lentils. There was no consensus; some liked it best with white beans, others black beans, and still others with lentils. Each one gives the soup a decidedly different flavor!

Black Bean Salad

Lentil Quinoa Salad

Hearty Salads

Tabbouleh Salad

Black Bean Salad**

Great any time of year, but especially nice over a bowl of lettuce for a quick meal on a hot day.

¼ cup red wine vinegar
¼ cup xv olive oil
Juice of ¼ lime (approx 1 tsp)
1 large clove garlic, minced (1 T)

1 each red, orange, and yellow sweet pepper, diced
½ large sweet white or red onion, chopped fine (¾ cup)
2 cups fresh raw corn cut off the cob (3-4 large ears)
4-5 cups black beans, drained

2-3 T Italian parsley, chopped fine

Mix first 4 ingredients for dressing and set aside.
Prepare the rest and pour dressing over all but the parsley.
Blend well, then mix in the parsley.
Leave on counter for 30 minutes, stirring up occasionally.
Stores in fridge for up to 5-6 days.

Creamy Pineapple Coleslaw**

Light, fresh, creamy, and oh so refreshing!

2 T vanilla soy yogurt
½ cup lightly drained crushed pineapple
2 cups green cabbage, shredded fine
Small pinch of cinnamon

Mix together yogurt, cinnamon, and pineapple. Stir in the cabbage.
Eat right away or chill for a couple hours.

Fresh Fruity Coleslaw**

Ah, the simple things in life are often the most enjoyable.

1 ¾ cups green cabbage, grated
¼ cup (or less) carrot, grated
1 ½ T 100% orange juice
1 ½ tsp pure maple syrup

Mix it all up and serve immediately.

Please note: This is especially good in late summer when the cabbage is fresh from the field. It is
   also good the next day, unlike some coleslaw. (Store any extra in a covered container in fridge.)

Fresh Cranberry Salad**

This is a nice light snack any time, or after a heavier meal.

3 cups (12 oz) fresh cranberries
1 large or 2 small empire apples
1 large orange
¼ cup honey

Thoroughly rinse all fruit.
Sort the cranberries to remove the ones with soft spots.
Core and quarter the apples.
Zest half the orange and place in a bowl. Remove the rest of the orange rind and discard.
Place the cranberries, apples, and orange into a food processor.
Pulse the fruit until approx ¼"-⅓" pieces.
Add this mixture to the bowl, then the honey and mix thoroughly.
Chill covered in the fridge for 2-8 hours, mixing every couple hours if you have the chance.
Fluff with a fork and serve.
Will keep in fridge several days.

Option: Replace honey with 2-3 T maple sugar or raw sugar.

Hearty Quinoa Salad**

This is great for quick lunches all week. It's light, but as Grandma would say, it sticks to your ribs!

2 cups quinoa
4 cups water

Dressing:
½ cup red wine vinegar
½ cup xv olive oil
1 T fresh lime juice
½ tsp whole salt
1 large clove garlic, minced (approx 1 T)

Veggies:
1 ½ sweet red peppers, diced in ½" pieces
3-4 scallions sliced thin, including the greens (¾-1 cup)
¼ cup fresh Italian parsley, chopped fine

Bring quinoa and water to a boil.
Cover and reduce heat to very low. Cook for 15 minutes until all water is absorbed.
Uncover and remove from heat.
While quinoa is cooling, wisk together the 5 ingredients of the dressing.
Chop veggies and place in a large bowl.
When quinoa is cool add to veggies, then thoroughly mix the dressing in.
If possible, leave on the counter for 30-60 minutes, mixing up every 15 minutes before storing in
   the fridge.

This salad has an even better flavor the next day.

Options:
- Add 1-2 cups black beans for an extra nutritional boost, and a nice contrast in the salad.
- If scallions are not available, replace with ½-¾ cup sweet onions, chopped fine.
- The ½ cup red wine vinegar can be replaced with cider vinegar and balsamic vinegar; start with
   a ratio of 6T cider vinegar to 2T balsamic vinegar. Depending on the type of balsamic, you can
   go as high as a ratio of ¼ cup cider vinegar and ¼ cup balsamic vinegar.
- This is a very light salad. If you prefer a more savory salad, increase the dressing to 1 ½ times the
   recipe and gradually mix in the extra to your own taste.

Lentil Quinoa Salad**

This makes a quick lunch for the week, or add a lettuce and veggie salad for a hearty dinner.

1 ½ cups brown lentils
4 ½ cups water

1 cup quinoa
2 cups water

Dressing:
½ cup xv olive oil
½ cup apple cider vinegar
1 T basil
½ T dill weed
1 tsp whole salt
1 large clove garlic, minced (1 T)

Veggies:
6 scallions with greens, sliced in ⅛" disks (1-1 ½ cups)
1 sweet green pepper, cleaned and diced into ½" pieces
1 sweet red pepper, cleaned and diced

1 large bunch Italian parsley, chopped fine (1 cup)

Bring lentils and water to a simmer, cover, turn down to medium low and cook for 20-35 minutes until the lentils are just cooked but not mushy.
Cool to room temperature and drain off any excess water.
Bring quinoa and water to a simmer, turn down to low, cover and cook for 15 minutes. Remove from heat. (If any liquid remains after 15 minutes, leave lid on for 5-10 minutes more.)
Fluff, and let cool to room temperature.
While the quinoa and lentils are cooling, whisk together the dressing and set aside.
Prepare the veggies in a large mixing bowl.
When all is cool, mix all but the dressing together, then thoroughly mix in the dressing.
Leave on the counter for 30-40 minutes stirring occasionally.
Cover and store in fridge for up to 6 days.
As with most grain/bean salads, it is even better the second day.

Note: Watch the lentils toward the end of the cooking as there's a short window between cooked and mush.

Options:

- Substitute the dry herbs with 3 T fresh basil and 1 ½ T fresh dill, both chopped fine.
- Replace the dill with 1 tsp dry/1 T fresh oregano.
- Green lentils are fine to use, too.

Rainbow Fruit Salad**

5-6 cups fresh fruit of your choice, diced
½ cup fresh orange juice
2 T raisins
Grated coconut: 1 T unsweetened dry, or 2 T fresh
1 T honey

One nice fruit combination is:
1 small peeled mango,
1 each apple, pear, orange,
1-2 cups strawberries,
1 cup blueberries,
2 pitted plums,
Several pitted cherries and seedless grapes.

Mix well and enjoy.

Option: Simply mix together the fruit and orange juice. The orange juice will keep the fruit from discoloring as quickly and will accent the fruit flavors.

Tabbouleh Salad**

When fresh tomatoes and cucumbers are available, this is hard to beat!

1 ¼ cups quinoa
2 ½ cups water

Dressing:
¼ cup xv olive oil
½ cup fresh lemon juice
¼ tsp fresh ground black pepper
¼ tsp whole salt
1 medium clove garlic, minced (½ T)

Veggies:
½ cup navy pea or black beans, drained (optional)
3 medium tomatoes, diced
¾ cup scallions with greens, sliced thin.
1 cucumber (⅔ of a burpless), diced
1 ½ cups Italian parsley, chopped fine

Bring quinoa and water to a simmer. Cover and cook on low 15 minutes.
(If all the water has not absorbed, leave lid on for 5-10 minutes before fluffing.)
Fluff up and pour into a bowl to cool.
Mix together the dressing and set aside.
Prepare the veggies and place in a large bowl.
Mix in the cooled quinoa, then the salad dressing.
If possible, leave at room temp for an hour, stirring occasionally.
Refrigerate for at least 2-3 hrs before serving.
Store in fridge for up to 6 days for a quick meal any time.

Herb Bread

Multi Seed Bread

Breads and Rolls

Fluffy Oatmeal Rolls

Cinnamon Rolls

These are a perennial favorite. The fragrance and taste of warm cinnamon rolls... oh my!

Oven temp: 350 degrees
Use the same dough and preparations as the Multi Seed Bread (p. 46) with a few alterations.
Increase honey to 1 cup and omit the seeds and millet.

Additional ingredients needed:
1 ½ cups raw sugar
6 T cinnamon
2 cups raisins

Mix together cinnamon and sugar and set aside.
Once dough has risen, divide into 6 equal pieces.
Preheat oven to 350.
Roll one piece out to 16"x 8" x ⅓" thick, with the edges away from you slightly wider.
Spread ⅓ cup cinnamon-sugar mixture evenly over the top and ½" from the edge.
Evenly sprinkle ⅓ cup raisins next.
Gently but snuggly roll up lengthwise 1" at a time, tucking in as you move left to right and right
    to left until you reach the edge. Pinch the edges and ends closed. Once pinched closed, gently
    stretch from the center out as needed to equalize the thickness of the roll.
Cut into 1" pieces and place cut side down on a greased cookie sheet approx 1" apart. (Each loaf
    makes 13-16 rolls.)
Bake: 350 for 14-16 minutes until rolls spring back when lightly pushed in the center and where
    the rolls touch.
Take out of the oven.

Removing the Rolls From the Cookie Sheet:
The rolls can rest 5-10 minutes then be removed one by one and placed on a cooling rack, or im-
    mediately place a cooling rack on top of the rolls and with pot holders carefully invert. Remove
    cookie sheet, place a second cooling rack on the bottom of the rolls, invert. Remove top rack and
    cool completely (or at least allow 10 minutes to set before eating).
Keep in the fridge for up to a week or freeze.

Options:

- As many of the 6 pieces as you like can be formed into plain loaves.

- Prefer cinnamon bread? Roll a piece of dough out to approx 8"x 10"x ⅔" thick. Add the same amount cinn/sugar and raisins as above and roll up the opposite way for a thick, 8" wide loaf. Pinch and place in an oiled loaf pan and bake as stated. Cinnamon raisin bread will take several minutes longer to bake than plain bread. It can also be baked on a baking stone but doesn't hold its shape as well because of the layers. Cool at least 30 minutes to set before slicing into fresh baked bread.

- 3-4 T honey mixed with 1 T cinnamon can be drizzled over the dough in place of the cinnamon-sugar mix.

Herb Bread

This is a nice change for sandwiches, and very tasty toasted!

4 cups lukewarm water	Herbs:
2 T yeast	4 tsp garlic powder
¼ cup honey	1 tsp rosemary
	1 T fresh parsley, chopped fine
¼ cup granular lecithin	¾ tsp oregano
6 T xv olive oil	1½ tsp thyme
4 tsp whole salt	1½ tsp basil
11-12 cups spelt flour (approx 3#)	1 large clove garlic, minced

In a large bowl, mix together the water, yeast and honey.

Then stir in the lecithin, oil, salt, and enough flour to make a thick mud.

Stir 100 times slowly (in the same direction). Let it sit for 20 minutes.

Mix in all the herbs, then enough flour to form a ball.

Pour onto a floured surface and knead 8-10 minutes until bounces back when dough is depressed with fingers.

Cover with a warm damp towel for 30-40 minutes until dough has risen 50%.

Divide into 4 loaves, gently knead each 10-12 times, and place on oiled baking stone, seams pinched, smooth side up.

Cover with a warm, damp towel for 5-10 minutes until loaves have risen about 25%.

Bake: 375 for 30-35 minutes until bottom of loaf is lower in pitch than the outside edge.

Cool completely on cooling rack.

Option: Except for the garlic and parsley, replace dried herbs with ½ cup packed fresh herbs.
(Basic rule of thumb: 1 tsp dry = 1 T fresh.)

Fluffy Oatmeal Rolls

For the times a soft, sweet roll is needed.

Preheat oven to 375 degrees

1 cup quick oats
3 T light olive oil
1 T granular lecithin
¼ cup honey
1 ¼ tsp whole salt

2 cups boiling water

⅓ cup lukewarm water
1 T active dry yeast

5-7 cups spelt flour

Mix together first 5 ingredients. Stir in the boiling water and let sit until room temperature.
Stir the yeast into ⅓ cup water until dissolved.
Add to mixture once cooled.
Gently stir in enough flour to form a soft ball.
Slowly and gently knead dough for 5-10 minutes until springs back when gently pushed.
Cover with a damp towel and let rise approx 40 minutes until almost doubles in size.
Form into 18 balls and place in a 13" x 9" ceramic baking dish greased with coconut oil. (6 rows of 3.)
    Cover with the damp towel for 5-7 minutes.
Bake: 375 degrees for 20-25 minutes until golden brown.
Remove from baking dish and cool on rack completely. (See page 42 for instructions for removing
    from the dish.)

Please note: Stirring dough in the same direction is recommended.

Multi Seed Bread

A great bread for sandwiches, with soup, or eating massive amounts by itself when still warm!

4 cups regular oats
2 cups whole grain flour
3 T plus ½ tsp whole salt
½ cup granular lecithin
½ cup light olive oil

¾ cup honey
8 cups boiling water

¼ cup active dry yeast
2 cups lukewarm water

10 cups hard red wheat flour
8-10 cups hard white wheat flour

1 ½ cups sunflower seeds
½ cup sesame seeds
½ cup millet

Mix together the first 6 ingredients in a huge bowl.

Mix the boiling water and honey together and stir into the first 6 ingredients.

Let cool to room temperature.

Mix the lukewarm water and yeast together and stir into the rest. (Stir in the same direction through the whole bread-making process—it makes the yeast happy.)

Slowly and gently, one cup at a time, add hard red flour until it is the consistency of thick mud. Gently stir 100 strokes to incorporate air into the dough.

Let sit for 20 minutes.

Stir in the seeds and millet.

Mix in the remaining hard red flour then enough hard white flour to form a ball.

Scrape out onto a floured surface and knead slowly and gently for 10 minutes, adding only enough flour on the surface and on your hands to keep dough from sticking. Dough should be soft but spring back when a couple fingers are pushed into it.

Oil the bowl used and place dough in smooth side down, then flip over. Cover with a warm damp towel and let sit for 35-45 minutes until the dough is approx half again as big.

Oil your hands and slowly punch down the dough 30 times. Cover again for 30-40 minutes to rise again.

Pour dough out onto a floured surface into a long shape.

Cut into 6 equal pieces. (Approx 2 ¼ # each.) Knead each piece several times then roll up into the desired shape.

Pinch the ends and place on an oiled baking stone (or loaf pan.)

When all are in loaves, cover with the towel to sit for 5-8 minutes to rise a bit.

Bake: 350 degrees for 34-44 minutes.

When loaves are nicely browned, carefully remove one loaf and flip over. Tap on the outside edge of the bottom, then the middle. The outside edge will be a high pitch, the middle will be a lower pitch if bread is done. If it is higher pitched, return to the oven and bake another 3-4 minutes before checking again. (If the bread isn't really firm when you start taking it off the stone, leave it for another 5 minutes or more.) You will get a feel for it after a few times. Remember somewhat over cooked bread still makes good toast and French toast, unlike undercooked.

Notes:
- The seeds may be omitted if you are interested in making cinnamon rolls as well as loaves of bread.
- Hard red and white flours are both 100% whole grain flours. Using all hard white will give you a lighter bread, but mixing with the hard red produces a nicer flavor.
- If you are short on baking time, or just want fresh bread 2 days in a row; divide up the dough, place each in an oiled plastic bag three times the size needed, seal and place in the fridge for up to 12 hours. Punch down in the bag, then rise 30-40 minutes before shaping into loaves.
- Remember dough rises more quickly on warm humid days than on cold damp days.

Quick Rye Bread

This bread is lighter and rises quicker thanks to the gluten and a small amount of unbleached flour. It is especially good toasted!

Oven temp: 350 degrees
8 cups lukewarm water
4 T active dry yeast
½ cup honey
⅓ cup granular lecithin

2 T whole salt
¼ cup light olive oil
¾ cup wheat gluten powder
½ cup caraway seeds

4 cups unbleached flour
16-18 cups fresh ground rye flour

2-3 more cups unbleached flour for kneading

Mix together the first 4 ingredients and let sit for 10 minutes.
Add the next 4 in the order listed.
Gradually add flour one cup at a time until it is the consistency of mud.
Gently stir 100 strokes then let rest for 20 minutes.
(Remember to stir the same direction while making bread.)
Continue to stir in flour until it forms a ball.
Roll out on a floured surface and gently and slowly knead for 8-10 minutes until dough springs
   back when gently pushed.
Cover with a damp towel and let rest for 45-75 minutes until it increases half again in size.
Divide into 4 pieces,
Knead each just a bit, form into round loaves and place on oiled round baking stones.

Above: Baked with only rye flour. Left: Baked with unbleached flour. It is puffier, but not as tasty as 100% rye flour!

Cover and let rest for another 10-20 minutes until dough has risen about 20%.

Slit tops ¼" down.

Bake: 350 degrees for 50-60 minutes.

To be sure it is baked, flip a loaf over, tap on side and center. The edge will be high pitched, and the center should be low pitched. If not, return to oven for another 5 minutes then check another loaf.

Right after setting loaves on a cooling rack, brush the loaves with ice cold water. Wait a minute and repeat 2 more times. This will soften the crust.

Cool completely before placing in bags.

Options:
- A thick cookie sheet may be used for baking. Shape into oval loaves and leave a minimum of 4" between loaves. This may reduce the baking time.
- Dough can be divided into 5 or 6 loaves and baking time will be reduced to 35-40 minutes.

Please note:
- Keep in mind the dough will rise quicker in warm humid weather, slower in cold damp weather.
- Be sure the rye flour is from whole, fresh ground rye berries.

Quick Sourdough Yeast Bread

This is a quick, light bread with a little sourdough taste.

Loaves bake at 375 degrees

Starter:
1 ½ cups lukewarm water
1T yeast
1 ½ cups spelt flour
6T honey

Bread dough:
1 ¾ cups lukewarm water
1T yeast
1 cup starter
1T honey
1 ½ tsp whole salt
¼ tsp baking soda
¼ cup granular lecithin
6-7 cups spelt flour

4 days ahead make starter:
Mix all the ingredients together. Leave out overnight uncovered.
(Mixture expands then contracts.)
In the morning, store covered in fridge until needed.
After waiting at least 4 days, it's ready to be used in bread.

In a large bowl gradually mix together the dough ingredients in the order listed.
Use enough flour to form into a ball.
Pour the dough onto a well floured surface and knead for 4-5 minutes until smooth and elastic.
Oil the bowl, place dough smooth side down and flip over.
Cover the bowl with a warm damp cloth for 35-45 minutes until 50% larger.

Divide into 2 loaves, knead just a bit and form into round or oval loaves.
Place on oiled bread stones.
Cover with oiled plastic wrap or damp towel and let rise 30-40 minutes until 25% larger.
Bake: 375 for 25-35 minutes until center of bottom sounds hollow.
Cool 30 minutes before slicing. Cool completely before storing.

Option:

- Braided loaf: Divide half the dough into 3 strips approx 10" long. Set the strips on the oiled baking stone, pinch the three ends, braid them together, pinch the other end, and fold the ends under just a bit. Bake as above.

- If you'd like a lighter loaf, replace a couple cups of the spelt flour with unbleached flour.

Shroom rolls

These are very popular with people...and dogs. After making them one day, I went upstairs for five, maybe ten minutes. Upon returning to the kitchen, the two large cookie sheets filled with rolls were in the exact same location, but completely empty; not even a crumb. After a closer look, a single, faint paw print could be seen on the edge of the counter. Looking down at the brother/sister lab conspirators, one was remorseful as usual, the other—the ring leader—had the usual look on her face: "Yeah, I did it. They're gone. Get over it... is there anything else to eat?"

These are good with dinner, or as a quick lunch—for humans!

Preheat oven to 375 degrees
2 cups lukewarm water
2T yeast
2 tsp honey
2T olive oil
1tsp whole salt
4-6 cups spelt flour

Filling:
¼ cup xv olive oil
8 large cloves garlic, chopped fine (yes, ⅓-½ cup garlic!)
8 cups (28 oz.) baby portabella mushrooms, sliced ¼" thick
½ tsp dill weed
A sprinkle of whole salt and black pepper (roughly ¼ tsp each)

Stir together water, yeast, and honey.
Wait a minute, then stir in oil, salt, and enough flour to form into a ball.
Gently and slowly knead on a floured surface (adding just enough flour to surface and hands to
    keep from sticking) for approx 10 minutes. Dough should spring back when pushed.
Return to oiled bowl and roll over to oil all sides.
Cover with warm, damp towel until almost doubled in size (30-40 minutes, depending on room
    temp and humidity).

Filling:
While waiting, prepare the filling.
Have all of the filling ingredients readily at hand.
Heat a thick-bottomed pan on high.
Add oil, then immediately add in mushrooms (shrooms), garlic, dill, salt and pepper.
Stir almost continually until shrooms are done. Set aside.

Divide dough into 2 pieces. Roll out 1 piece to 8"x15".

Spread half of shroom filling evenly over dough.

Roll up snuggly lengthwise (without tearing dough), tucking right to left, left to right until all rolled up. Pinch all edges closed.

Cut in 1 ¼" pieces, pinching together the open ends as best you can—especially the top.

Place on an oiled cookie sheet.

Bake at 375 for 18-24 minutes, until dough springs back when pressed and bottoms are browned.

Cool on cooling rack.

Starter For Traditional Sourdough Bread

2 cups lukewarm water
2 cups whole grain flour

Combine flour and water in a non-metallic bowl or glass quart mason jar, stirring with a non-metallic spoon.
Let it sit uncovered for 2-5 days in a warm place, such as a windowsill with the window open. (Screened of course to keep insects out!)
Stir occasionally.
When ready, the mixture will have a clean, yeasty smell with little bubbles, and will be stickier than before.
Cover tightly and keep your new starter in the fridge until needed.
Use within 2 ½ weeks or add ¼ cup more each of water and flour.
Set on windowsill again for 6-8 hours and return to fridge.

Traditional Sourdough Bread

A dense, hearty bread that is especially good toasted.
Use only non-metalic bowls and utensils with sourdoughs.

Previously made "traditional starter'" (2 - 2 ½ cups)

Add to starter:
4 cups kamut flour
4 cups lukewarm water

Remove starter from fridge and add the above 4 cups each of flour and water.
Cover and leave on counter overnight for 12-18 hours until it has a foamy/bubbly look.
In the morning, mix well and reserve 2 cups in an open container for the rest of the day.
(Close securely and return to fridge by evening.)

Bread dough:

4 cups lukewarm water
¼ cup honey
¼ cup xv olive oil
⅓ cup granular lecithin
4 tsp whole salt
A 2:1 or 1:1 ratio of kamut and spelt flour (15-20 cups total)

1-2 cups chopped almonds and pecans

Pour the remaining starter into a large mixing bowl.
Stir in water, honey, oil, lecithin, and enough of the flour mixture to make a thick mud.
Gently stir 100 times in the same direction.
Let sit for 20 minutes, then stir in the nuts.
Gradually stir in enough additional flour mixture to form a ball.
Roll out onto a floured counter, and knead gently and slowly for 10 minutes.
Place back into the oiled bowl, flip over to oil both sides, and cover with a warm damp towel.
Leave in a warm draft-free place for 2-3 hours until almost double in size.
Divide into 4 or 5 loaves and knead 6-8 times, pinching the bottom together.
Set on oiled baking stone smooth side up, cover with a warm damp towel and let sit for about 1
   hour until almost 50% larger.
Slice the top a couple times ¼" deep.
Bake at 350 for 45-60 minutes depending on how many loaves you have.
They should be lightly browned on top, and the bottom tapped should be high pitched on the
   edge, low pitched in the middle.
As soon as the loaves are placed on a cooling rack, brush with ice water twice if you like a softer
   crust.
Cool completely before placing in bags.

Please note: Wait 3 days before re-using the starter. If not used again after 20 days, stir in ¼ cup
   flour and ¼ cup lukewarm water. Place opened on window sill all day and back in fridge at
   night. Wait again 3 days before using.
If you let the starter go a bit too long or you're just in a hurry, 1 T of yeast can be added to the bread
   dough water. This will cut the 1st rising time down to as little as 1 hour; 2nd to 15-25 minutes..

Mongo Banana Muffins

Yammers

Quick Breads

Hearty Cornbread

Fluffy Drop Biscuits

Fluffy whole grain biscuits!? No, I'm not kidding. And for those of you who are not "old as dirt" as my children lovingly refer to me on occasion, a drop biscuit is just that, the dough dropped on the cookie sheets in even amounts. These are great for strawberry shortcake, with a little honey, or plain just out of the oven with your favorite buttery spread.

Preheat oven to 400 degrees

2 cups spelt flour
2 cups kamut flour
2 T baking powder
1 ¼ tsp whole salt

1 ½ cups plain soy milk
1 T apple cider vinegar
1 tsp vanilla extract
2 tsp honey

½ cup light olive oil

Mix together flour, baking powder, and salt. Cut in the oil with a pastry cutter until small crumbles.
Separately mix together milk, vinegar, vanilla, and honey.
Let it set for a couple minutes.
Fold the wet gently and slowly into the dry until just moistened.
Let it rest for 5 minutes.
Spoon the batter onto a greased, thick bottomed cookie sheet approx 3" wide x 1"high and 2" apart.
Bake: 400 degrees for 10-12 minutes until toothpick comes out clean and a medium brown color on the bottom. Let rest a couple minutes before eating.
Cool remaining biscuits completely on cooling rack and store in airtight container in fridge for up to 3 days.

Options:
- Use vanilla soy milk and omit the vanilla and honey.
- Salt may be reduced to 1 tsp.
- If all spelt flour is used additional flour will be needed, as kamut flour is denser.
- For round biscuits, add enough extra flour to easily fold in half & flatten out to 1 inch or so several times. Then press down gently to 1" thick, & cut out with a 2 ½" - 3" round biscuit cutter. Bake as above.

Hearty Cornbread*

This goes well with burritos and salad.

Preheat oven to 375 degrees

Dry Ingredients:
½ cup spelt flour
½ cup kamut flour
¾ cup fine ground cornmeal
½ T baking powder
½ tsp baking soda
½ tsp whole salt
2 T fresh ground flax seeds

Wet Ingredients:
1 cup plain soy milk mixed with:
1 T apple cider vinegar
¼ cup maple syrup (or honey)
¼ cup light olive oil
2 T ground sesame seeds

Mix the wet and dry in separate bowls, then gradually add the dry into the wet until all is just
    moistened. Let mixture sit for 5-10 minutes while oiling a 9" pie plate. Pour in batter.
Bake in preheated oven 20-25 minutes until toothpick inserted in the center comes out clean.
Cool on cooling rack 10-15 minutes to set before serving.

Gluten Free Option: This is so good, I considered making it the primary recipe. Substitute spelt
    and kamut flour with: 2 cups chickpea flour and 2 T brown rice flour. Increase maple syrup by
    1T, and add ½ tsp arrowroot powder. All the rest is the same. This produces a wonderfully light
    corn bread!

Mongo Banana Muffins

These muffins require a few more ingredients than the other banana muffin recipe but will keep you going far longer.

Preheat oven to 375 degrees

1 cup spelt flour
1 cup kamut flour
½ cup oat bran
¼ tsp whole salt
½ tsp baking soda
2 tsp baking powder
2 T ground flax seed
½ cup chopped pecans

¼ cup light olive oil
½ cup unsulphured molasses
1 T ground sesame seeds
½ T soaked chia seeds (see below)
1 tsp vanilla extract
½ cup plain soy milk mixed with 1 tsp apple cider vinegar
1 ¼ cups mashed, ripe bananas

Mix dry ingredients together in one bowl.
Mix wet ingredients together in a different large bowl.
Gently and gradually stir the dry ingredients into the wet ingredients until just moist.
Let sit for 7-8 minutes. If not a thick but soft consistency, add more flour or pureed banana as
   needed.
Grease a 12-cup muffin tin with coconut oil.
Spoon the batter into each cup until the batter almost fills the cup.
Bake: 375 for 12-15 minutes until a toothpick inserted in the center comes out clean and batter-
   free.
Cool muffins in tin for 10 minutes.
Gently roll muffins out onto a cooling rack and leave until completely cool.
Eat within 24 hours or freeze in air-tight freezer bag.

Soaked chia seeds: Place ½ T chia seeds in ¼ cup water. Cover and store in the fridge for 8 hours
   or overnight. (Shake up occasionally if possible.)

Quick Banana Muffins

These are amazingly light and delicious. Kids of all ages love them.

Preheat oven to 375 degrees

1 cup spelt flour
1 cup kamut flour
3 T ground flax seeds
1 tsp baking powder
½ tsp baking soda
½ tsp whole salt

⅓ cup light olive oil
⅓ cup honey
¼ cup plain soy milk mixed with:
    1 tsp apple cider vinegar

1 ¼ cups bananas, well ripened and well mashed (roughly 3 bananas)

Mix the dry ingredients together. Mix the wet ingredients together.
Slowly and gently mix the dry into the wet just until all is moistened.
Let sit for 5-7 minutes while greasing a 12 count muffin tin with coconut oil.
Fill the cups even or a bit above the top.
Bake: 375 degrees for 14-16 minutes until a toothpick inserted in the center comes out clean.
Set on cooling rack 10 minutes before removing from the tin, then watch them disappear!

Options: Add ½ cup chopped pecans or ½ cup chocolate chips. The excess batter from adding
   these makes 8-10 mini muffins, which take 8-10 minutes to bake.

Please note: Use bananas that are so speckled the specks start connecting, but not to the point of
   molding of course.

Spicy Gingerbread

This is so good any time of day. Nutritious enough for a quick meal, sweet enough for dessert.

Preheat oven to 350 degrees

Dry ingredients:
1 cup kamut flour
1 cup spelt flour
1 tsp baking soda
½ tsp whole salt
1 ½ tsp cinnamon
1 tsp ginger
¼ tsp clove

Wet ingredients:
⅓ cup olive oil
1 cup plain soy milk mixed with 1 Tbls apple cider vinegar
1 cup unsulfured molasses
2 T ground flax seeds

Mix together the first 7 dry ingredients.
In a large bowl mix together the 4 wet ingredients.
Slowly add the dry into the wet until just moistened.
Let sit for 5-7 minutes, then check consistency of the batter. It should be on the thick side. If it seems too thin, add 1 or 2 T more of flour.
Oil a 9x9" baking dish with coconut oil, pour in batter.
Bake: 350 degrees for 35-45 minutes, until toothpick inserted in center comes out clean.
Set on cooling rack for at least 15 minutes before serving.

Options:
- Replace flax seeds with 1 ½ T chia seeds soaked in 6 T water for several hours or overnight.
- Replace soy milk with almond milk.

Tropical Zucchini Bread

This recipe is moist and flavorful with a lot less oil than other zucchini recipes.
Very satisfying any time of day.

Preheat oven to 350 degrees

Dry ingredients:
1 cup spelt flour
1 cup kamut flour
1 ½ tsp cinnamon
2 tsp baking soda
½ tsp whole salt
½ cup pecans, chopped

Wet ingredients:
⅓ cup light olive oil
⅔ cup applesauce
3 T ground flaxseed
1 tsp vanilla extract
⅔ cup maple sugar
1 cup crushed pineapple well drained
⅓ cup pineapple juice as needed
2 ½ cups zucchini; cored, shredded and packed

Mix together first 6 ingredients.
In large separate bowl mix the next 8 ingredients and let sit for 10 minutes.
Slowly and gently stir the dry into the wet until just moistened.
Grease 2 loaf pans with coconut oil, pour the batter evenly between the two.
Bake: 350 degrees for 30-40 minutes until toothpick comes out clean.
Cool on cooling rack for 10 minutes then remove from pans to cool completely.

Options:
- Batter will also make approx 12 regular sized muffins and 12 mini muffins. Fill to a little above the top. Bake 18-22 and 8-12 minutes respectively.
- 2 cups of packed shredded carrots can be added in place of the zucchini for good carrot cake or muffins.

Yammers*

These biscuits are loved by all ages!

Preheat oven to 375 degrees, moving rack one up from middle.

Dry ingredients:
1 cup spelt flour
1 cup kamut flour
1 T baking powder
½ tsp whole salt

Wet ingredients:
¾ cup prepared yams*
¼ cup light olive oil
¼ cup maple syrup
½ tsp vanilla
¼ cup plain soy milk
½ tsp apple cider vinegar

Mix dry ingredients together and set aside.
Beat together the wet ingredients, mixing the milk and vinegar together for a minute before adding to the rest.
Slowly stir the dry into the wet until just moistened.
Let it rest for 5 minutes.
Scrape into a soft ball, using a little more flour as needed.
Roll out onto a floured surface. Flatten out only enough to be able to fold in half.
Gently repeat the process 6 or 7 more times.
Gently flatten out to about ¾" thick, cut into 2" diameter rounds with a biscuit cutter.
Place 2" apart on a greased, thick bottomed cookie sheet.
Bake: 375 degrees for 10-14 minutes, until center springs back when slightly depressed, or a toothpick comes out clean. (Err on the more cooked side.)
Cool completely on cooling rack.

*Yams: Bake at least 2 medium yams, 350 degrees, 30 minutes 1st side, prick with a fork, flip over and bake approx 30 minutes more until soft. (Cover cookie sheet with foil and oil lightly for easy clean-up.) When cool enough, peel, push through a potato ricer, then measure out the ¾ cup. Can prepare the day before, if preferred. Cook extra, as they freeze well for future batches.

Gluten Free Option: Replace dry ingredients with: 1 cup chickpea flour, 1T xanthan gum powder, 1 tsp brown rice flour, ½ cup sorghum flour, ¼ cup millet flour, 1 T ground flax seeds, 1T baking powder, ½ tsp whole salt, and extra sorghum flour for folding at the end. The taste and texture is almost identical!

Other Options:
- You can substitute honey for maple syrup.
- Drained canned yams may be substituted.

Please note: They can be baked at a little higher temp, but not lower. They should be soft but flakey when completely cooked. Enjoy just as they are, or sliced in half with some of your favorite buttery spread... mmm.

Coconut Bars

Honey Roasted Nuts

Snacks

Easy Crunchy Crackers

Coconut Bars**

These are simply great! Light, sweet, and very quick to make.

Dry mix options:

Option 1:
2 ½ cups dry, unsweetened coconut flakes
⅔ cup almonds, chopped fine
2 ½ T sesame seeds, brown unhulled

Option 2:
2 cups dry, unsweetened coconut flakes
¾ cup almonds, chopped fine

Syrup:
¾ tsp xv coconut oil
¾ tsp liquid lecithin
1 ½ T tahini
2 T honey
2 T maple syrup
½ tsp vanilla

Option 3:
2 cups dry, unsweetened coconut flakes
½ cup almonds, chopped fine
2 T sesame seeds, brown unhulled

Mix together the dry ingredients option of your choice and set aside.
Heat a thick bottom, nonstick 12" fry pan on low.
Drop the syrup ingredients into the pan in the order listed.
Raise the temp to medium high stirring constantly.
Once it begins to softly bubble, stir another minute. (If it starts to darken, the temp is too high.)
Sprinkle the dry ingredients evenly over syrup.
Stir and fold together for 3-5 minutes until well incorporated, no longer clumpy, and just slightly
  browned in some spots.
Immediately pour into an 8"x 8" baking dish lined with parchment paper.
With a second piece of paper press down very firmly, then cool until slightly warm.
With a pastry cutter, cut straight down into 2" squares.
Cool completely before storing in an airtight container.

Option: For a crispier bar reduce the tahini to 1 T and allow to brown just a tiny bit more.

Easy Crunchy Crackers

Don't be fooled by the short ingredient list. These crackers are the best, with several variations to please everyone.

Preheat oven to 400 degrees and set a smooth pizza stone in it to warm up
½ cup oat flour
1 cup barley flour (more for rolling out)
¾ cup spelt flour
1 ¼ tsp whole salt
¾ cup warm water
Toasted sesame seeds, cumin seeds, etc.

Blend together the flours and salt.
Stir in water with a fork until it forms a ball. (Add more barley flour if too sticky)
Gently and slowly knead for 5 minutes.
Cover with a damp towel and let it sit for 10-60 minutes. It will be a heavy dense dough.
Cut into 4 pieces and place back under the damp towel.
One piece at a time flatten out with floured fingers enough to add ½ tsp seeds.
Fold over and proceed to gently knead the seeds into dough.
Flatten out with floured fingers to about ⅓" thick.
Making sure there is ample flour underneath, roll out to ¹⁄₃₂"- ¹⁄₁₆" thick (the thinner, the crispier).
Lightly sprinkle with salt and roll again to press the salt into the dough.
Remove the pizza stone from the oven and carefully slide the dough onto it.
Cut into 2" squares. (A pizza cutter works nicely.)
Bake 7-10 minutes, until crackers are hard to the touch and slightly browned.
Cool completely on cooling rack before storing in an airtight container... if there's any left.

Options:
- Replace all the flour with 100% fresh ground rye flour and add 2 tsp caraway or sesame seeds with the dry ingredients.
- Replace all the flours with ¾ cup oat flour, 1 cup barley flour, ½ cup buckwheat flour. Seeds can be added as stated above or rolled into the top with a sprinkle of salt.

Honey Roasted Nuts**

These are always popular when I've taken them places, and joyously received when given as a gift.

Preheat oven to 300 degrees

3 T light olive oil
6 T honey
1 T liquid lecithin
½ tsp whole salt
¼ tsp baking soda

1 cup almonds
1 ½ cups pecans
1 ½ cups walnuts

¾ tsp chili powder

Whisk together oil through soda until turns a lighter creamy color.
Mix in the nuts and spread out onto a large cookie sheet with sides.
Bake: 300 degrees for 7 minutes.
Stir up, spread out, and bake another 7 minutes, until the mixture between the nuts is just a little brown.
Set on a cooling rack, sprinkle the chili powder over the top and mix together thoroughly.
Every 5 minutes stir up the nuts until they cool completely.
Store in an airtight container.

Please note:
- If the mixture has not browned a bit at the end of the cooking time it will not set, if left in even a minute too long may burn.
- In a warm humid area these need to be put in the fridge as soon as cooled. In a cool dry area they can be left in a jar on the counter for a week or so.
- Be sure to add the chili powder AFTER baking. For those with a spicy palette, use 1 tsp chili powder.
- These may sound a little fussy to make, but once you find the right combination of times for your oven, they are one of the quickest and easiest snacks to make.

Kale Crisps**

1 bunch kale, ribs removed
1-2 T xv olive oil
½ tsp whole salt

Juice of ½ a small lemon (½ T plus)
½ T honey
¼ tsp garlic powder

After removing the tough center rib, tear the kale into roughly 2"x2" pieces.
Pour over kale: 1T oil, salt and lemon juice. Massage into kale for 3-4 minutes.
If the oil doesn't cover all the kale massage in a bit more.
Pour ½ T honey over kale and massage in also. (The mixture will have shrunk by almost 50%.)
The kale should taste good at this stage. Add a bit more salt or lemon juice as your taste buds
  dictate.
Dehydrate in your dehydrator at 115 degrees for approx 8 hours until just crispy.
Cool completely and store in an airtight container in a cool dry place.

Options: Bake in a 275 degree oven on cookie sheets stirring every 10 minutes until crispy.
Note: Kales vary considerably in flavor. Try several (such as Red Russian) to find your favorite.
Note also: Lemon and honey are optional.

Nutty Seed Brittle**

No oven involved; these are a delicious, nutritious, super quick snack.

Mix #1
½ cup sunflower seeds
¼ cup pumpkin seeds
¼ cup sesame seeds, brown unhulled
¼ cup pecans, chopped very fine

Mix #2
¾ cup sunflower seeds
¼ cup sesame seeds, brown unhulled
¼ cup pecans, chopped very fine

Syrup
½ tsp xv coconut oil
½ tsp liquid lecithin
1 T tahini
4 tsp honey
4 tsp maple syrup

Mix #3
⅔ cup pistachios, coarsely chopped
½ cup sunflower seeds
¼ cup pecans, chopped very fine
2 T sesame seeds

Cover a large cookie sheet with a piece of parchment paper, and have a second piece at hand.

Mix together seeds and nuts from one of the mixtures listed and set aside.

Place a 15" nonstick fry pan on low. Add syrup ingredients in order listed, placing them all in the same spot. Increase burner temp to medium/high, stirring constantly. Stir for 1-2 minutes until nice and bubbly. (If syrup darkens more than just slightly, the pan is too hot.)

Stir in the seeds and nuts, stirring and flipping for 2-4 minutes until a bit fragrant.

Pour onto parchment paper and spread out a bit using the edge of the spatula. Put the second piece of paper over the top and roll out with a rolling pin to a thin layer. Remove top paper, cool completely, break up into pieces and store in an airtight container. In hot/humid weather, store in the fridge.

Options:
- For those who like more of a sweet/salty flavor, ⅛ tsp salt may be added.
- For a more toasted flavor, the sunflower seeds may be dry roasted in the pan on medium high for 1-3 minutes before making the syrup, then added in with the rest of the nuts. (Stir them as they roast.)

- If your fry pan is any smaller, make half a recipe at a time for better results. Half the recipe cooked in the larger pan will produce crispier brittle.

For Bars:
Line an 8"x 8" baking dish with parchment paper, pour in mixture and press down very firmly. When still partially warm, pressing down with a pastry cutter, cut into 1 ½" squares.

Note: Measuring out such small amounts of the syrup ingredients can be a bit challenging. Better to have a little more than less in all but the tahini, which may reduce the crunchiness if too much.

P.B. Rollers**

These are great for all ages, and a filling ready-made snack for those who are always hungry.

⅔ cup oat bran
1 T flax seeds
1 cup raisins
⅓ cup sunflower seeds

2 cups natural, 100% peanut butter
6 T honey

1-1 ½ cups brown unhulled sesame seeds

Stir together the four dry ingredients.
Mix together the honey and 1 cup of PB, and stir into the dry.
Stir in enough of the second cup of PB to form a soft, firm dough that is not dry.
Form into 1" (or less) balls.
Roll in sesame seeds to cover.
Place in an airtight container in fridge until needed. (They will keep several weeks.)

Power Bars**

These are great to keep in the freezer when you need a quick, filling, but sweet snack.

Dry Ingredients:
⅓ cup brown unhulled sesame seeds
2 T ground sesame seeds
1 ½ cups walnuts, chopped
¾ cup old fashioned oats
¾ cup quick oats
⅓ cup oat bran
1 cup raisins, coarsely chopped
⅓ cup ground almonds
1 cup pecans, chopped
⅓ cup sliced almonds, broken up
⅓ cup raw sunflower seeds

Syrup:
¾ cup brown rice syrup
¼ cup honey
2 tsp vanilla extract
½ tsp whole salt
2 T liquid lecithin
¼ tsp baking soda

Oil a 13" x 9" baking dish with coconut oil.
In a large bowl mix all the dry ingredients together.
Mix the first 5 syrup ingredients in a sauce pan and bring to a simmer stirring constantly.
Simmer and stir another 1-2 minutes.
Take off the heat, and stir in the baking soda. (It will bubble up.) Pour over dry ingredients.
Quickly stir together with a large rigid spoon until very well mixed. (Wooden spoons work well.)
Pour into the 13" x 9" dish and press down very firmly.
Cool completely, cover, and let set a couple hours before cutting into. Keep in fridge in hot/humid
   weather.

Note: Cover the bars with wax paper to more easily compress them. The more compacted, the
   better they hold together.

Options:
- Omit honey for a bar not quite as sweet.
- Substitute the raisins for ¾ cup chopped dates.

Suet, A Snack For Birds

If you like to feed the birds but have no interest in having a caged piece of cow fat hanging outside your window, this is for you!

4 cups unbleached flour
2 cups margarine
2 tsp whole salt
¾ -1 cup ice water
1-2 cups birdseed (optional)

Spread 1 cup flour in large bowl. Sprinkle the salt on top. Add a second cup of flour.
Cut margarine into 1T pieces and add.
Pour the rest of the flour in.
Now roll your sleeves up and squish it all together.
When well mixed, add ¾ cup ice water at first and mix in with your fingers, adding more as needed until the consistency of pastry dough.
Mix in the birdseed last.

Not interested in exercising your fingers? Place in an extra large stationary mixer with the dough hook attachment and blend, in the order stated.

Form into rectangles that will fit in your suet cage, wrap in wax paper, pack them in a freezer bag, and store in your freezer until you need more suet.

It's comfort food for the birds. They love it!

Blueberry Crumble

Carob Mint Cake

Desserts

P. B. Carob Fudge

Apple Crisp Bake

A light, fresh dessert that is quicker to make than pie, with twice as many servings.

Preheat oven: 375 degrees

1 T light olive oil
1 ½ cups apple cider

1 cup quick oats
½ cup wheat germ
½ cup spelt flour
½ cup maple sugar
1 T cinnamon
¼ tsp whole salt

8-12 baking apples

3 T spelt flour
1 ½ tsp cinnamon

½ cup light olive oil

Drizzle the 1 T oil in the bottom of a high sided 10"x15" baking dish.
Pour in the cider and set aside.
Mix together oats through salt and set aside.
Peel, core, and slice apples about ¼" thick, filling a large Pyrex mixing bowl almost to the top.
Stir together the 3 T spelt and 1 ½ tsp cinnamon, pour over the apples and blend (scooping down
    from the outside edge up the center keeps it in the bowl).
Pour into baking dish, lightly packing apples while leveling out the top.
Stir the ½ cup oil into the oat mix and spread evenly over the apples, lightly pressing in place.
Bake: 375 degrees uncovered for 35-45 minutes, until a thin serving fork inserted in apples re-
    leases easily, indicating apples are done and top is lightly browned.
Let it cool and set a minimum of 30 minutes before serving.

Options:
- Substitute maple sugar with raw sugar.
- Replace the ½ cup wheat germ with ¾ cup oat bran.
- ¼ cup coarsely chopped walnuts can be added to the topping.
- Crispin or Northern Spy apples are my favorite for pies or crisp. Any dense, hearty apple that stands up to baking will do.

Note: If there is any left at the end of the day cover tightly, put in the fridge, or leave on the counter a couple days for the nibblers.

Baklava

This is such a sweet, nutty, rich dessert for special occasions, or any time.

Preheat oven to 350 degrees

1# phyllo dough, thawed and kept covered with a damp towel.

Syrup:
1 cup water
1 cup honey
1 cup raw sugar
1 or 2 – 3" cinnamon sticks

Filling:
1 ¼ # walnuts (5 cups), chopped fine
¼ cup raw sugar
1 tsp cinnamon

3-4 sticks melted soy margarine as needed (1½-2 cups)

To make the syrup, place in a small pan: water, honey, 1 cup sugar, and cinnamon sticks.
Stir continually as you bring to a medium simmer and then simmer for 5 minutes, cool to room temperature and remove cinnamon sticks.
Mix together nuts, ¼ cup sugar, and cinnamon. Set aside.
Put 3 sticks margarine in a saucepan on low. Once melted, use a pastry brush to "butter" the bottom and sides of a 10" x 15" x 2" baking dish.
On your counter, carefully spread out one layer of phyllo, brush half with margarine, fold over, brush top, and place in baking dish. (Should nicely fill bottom.) Repeat with 4 more sheets.
Sprinkle ½ cup nut mix evenly over top and cover with another sheet of buttered phyllo.
Repeat until all nut mix is used adding 6 more buttered phyllo sheets to the top.
Using a very sharp thin knife, carefully cut all the way through to the bottom in 2" square or diamond shapes.
Bake: 350 for 45-55 minutes, until medium golden brown.
Place on cooling rack, and pour room temperature syrup evenly over top. (It will puff up a bit.)
Let completely cool before serving. Eat in 2-3 days.

Please note: Phyllo dough dries out so quickly it needs to be kept covered with a lightly damp towel, even the short time between buttering sheets.

Baklava freezes very well, which is a good thing, because it is SO rich.
Share with friends and still have enough to freeze to enjoy later.

Blueberry Crumble**

This is so light and refreshing, with just the right amount of crunch on the top!

Preheat oven to 375 degrees

1 T light olive oil
1 T maple syrup
1 T arrowroot powder

4 cups blueberries

⅔ cup quick oats
¼ cup oat bran
¼ tsp cinnamon

2 T light olive oil
2 T maple syrup

Whisk together the first 3 ingredients.
Pour over the blueberries and fold together.
Pour into a lightly oiled 8"x 8" baking dish and set aside.
Mix together the oats, bran, and cinnamon.
Separately whisk together the oil and syrup, pour over the oat mixture and mix thoroughly.
Sprinkle the topping evenly over the blueberries.
Bake: 375 for 20-25 minutes, until sides are bubbly and center just starts to bubble.
Let cool 20-30 minutes before serving.

Options:
- If using frozen berries, will take 10-15 minutes longer to cook.
- For a 13x9 baking dish, double the recipe, and increase baking time a bit more.
- Any combination of berries may be used.
- For tarter fruits, such as thimbleberries/blackberries, increase the maple syrup in the fruit to 2 T.

Caramel Corn**

This has been a huge hit for a couple decades, by the young, and young at heart!

Preheat oven to 200 degrees.

8 quarts air popped popcorn
½ # (2 sticks) non-hydrogenated soy margarine
2 cups raw sugar
¼ cup honey

1 tsp whole salt
1 tsp baking soda
1 tsp vanilla extract

Place popcorn in a very large roasting pan.
Measure out the salt and baking soda in a small dish and have the vanilla and measuring spoon ready.
Add the margarine, sugar and honey to a large high sided pan, and bring to a simmer on medium heat stirring very frequently.
Increase to medium high stirring constantly until bubbly. Continue stirring for 5 minutes.
Remove from the heat and IMMEDIATELY pour in the vanilla, salt and soda, stir briskly for 20-30 seconds until smoother and creamier looking, then IMMEDIATELY pour onto the popcorn and mix until coated.
It will take 2-3 minutes to mix in evenly, stirring from the outside, down and up the center.
Bake at 200 degrees for 40 minutes, removing from the oven and stirring up every 10 minutes.
Spread out onto overlapping wax paper (covering an area 3 ½' x 2') until completely cooled.
Store in an air tight container for up to a week.

WARNING: Hot caramel really burns. I recommend wearing oven mitts while stirring the syrup into the popcorn. The syrup will bubble up when the baking soda is added then quickly hardens, which is why the last couple steps need to be accomplished quickly. It takes a bit to get the hang of it, but well worth it. Not to be made in humid weather though; the second it cools it begins to take on moisture.

Carob Mint Cake

When my kids were pretty young I introduced this to their friends as just "mint cake" and they loved it! There's just something about mixing mint and roasted carob together that gives it a more pronounced chocolate flavor.

Preheat oven to 350 degrees

Wet ingredients:
½ cup light olive oil
1 ½ tsp pure vanilla extract
1 ½ tsp apple cider vinegar
1 ¼ cups water
1 cup local raw honey
1 tsp peppermint extract
⅔ cup grated dark red beet, rough top skin removed; or ⅔ cup beet pulp from juicing beets.

Dry ingredients:
1 ¼ cups spelt flour
1 cup kamut flour
½ cup sifted ROASTED carob powder
¾ tsp whole salt
1 ½ tsp baking soda

Mix wet ingredients well.
Mix dry ingredients well in separate bowl.
Gently and gradually stir in dry ingredients, just until all are moistened.
It will be this weird brownish pinkish color, but it bakes into a rich dark brown color.
Consistency will be a little thinner than other cake batters.
Let sit for 5-10 minutes.
Lightly fold top to bottom a couple times.
Pour into a greased 13" x 9" glass or ceramic baking dish.
Bake: 350 for approx 25-30 minutes until toothpick inserted in the center comes out clean.
Cool on rack for at least 30 minutes to set. Cover tightly when completely cooled.

Options:
- Omit beet pulp and increase water to 1 ½ cups. Still good, but not the same melt-in-your-mouth moist!
- Replace carob powder with ½ cup sifted cocoa powder, and omit peppermint extract if you wish.

Creamy Rice Pudding**

Rich, creamy, and ridiculously easy to make!

7 cups plain soy milk
3 cups water
2 cups short (or medium) grain brown rice
⅔ cup maple syrup
¼ tsp whole salt
1 T vanilla extract

Mix all the ingredients in a medium size crock pot. (It may look like way too much liquid, but it will absorb into the rice.)
Cover and cook on low for 7-8 hours, stirring after 3, 5, and 7 hours.
After that, peek through the top to see when the pudding looks slightly wetter than you'd like it.
Stir well to check consistency, and test rice to make sure it is fully cooked.
Remove from the heat, with the lid just slightly ajar. (It absorbs more of the liquid as it cools.)
Cool completely and store in the fridge for up to 5 days.

Sweet enough for dessert, hearty enough for a quick lunch on the go!

Please note:
- The shorter grains have a nicer consistency than long grain in pudding.
- Honey can be substituted for the maple syrup.
- If the pudding isn't creamy enough once it cools, gradually stir in water ¼ cup at a time until desired consistency.
- If you use almond milk instead of soy milk, omit the salt and reduce the milk by 1 cup, to be added in at the end if needed for the proper consistency.
- ½ cup raisins can be added once the pudding has finished cooking.

Fudgy Brownies**

Whether gluten free or with spelt flour, these are downright addicting!

Preheat oven to 350 degrees

Dry ingredients:

⅓ cup sorghum flour
1 ½ T potato starch
1 T brown rice flour
¾ tsp arrowroot powder
3 T ground flaxseeds
⅛ tsp xanthan gum powder
⅛ tsp whole salt
½ cup unsweetened cocoa powder

Wet ingredients:

⅓ cup soft ripe avocado, mashed well (¾ of a small avocado)
1 T tahini
1 ½ tsp vanilla
½ tsp apple cider vinegar
⅔ cup maple syrup
¼ cup xv coconut oil, liquefied and still warm

Wisk dry ingredients together well and set aside.
In a large bowl blend the wet ingredients together one at a time in the order listed with an electric mixer until creamy.
Gradually blend in the dry ingredients. (If your mixer does not have a slow setting, begin to mix together with the beaters off, then blend on a higher and higher setting until the mixture is smooth and creamy.)
Let the batter set for 3-5 minutes to obtain a thicker but still smooth consistency.
Spread evenly into a 9"x 9" or 8"x 8" baking dish greased with coconut oil.
Bake: 350 for 15-20 minutes until toothpick comes out completely clean.
Cool on cooling rack. They will be fully set once they are cool.

Options:

- Replace sorghum, potato starch, rice flour, arrowroot powder and xanthan gum with ½ cup spelt flour.

- Replace cocoa powder with ½ cup roasted carob powder and ⅛ tsp peppermint (or almond) extract.

- Can increase the sorghum flour to ½ cup for a little less fudgy brownie.

- Can use ¼ cup kamut flour and ¼ spelt flour in place of the ½ cup spelt.

Nutty Cranberry Bars

The distinct flavor of the cranberries mixed with the oats makes a wonderful treat!

Crust:

Pre-heat oven to 350 degrees

1½ cups spelt flour
¼ cup maple sugar
¼ tsp baking soda
¼ tsp whole salt
1 ½ cups quick oats
¼ tsp arrowroot powder

¼ cup warm honey
⅔ cup light olive oil

½ cup chopped pecans

Cranberry Filling:

Make a day in advance

¾ cup water
1 cup pure maple syrup
3 cups fresh cranberries

Make the filling a day in advance:

Mix water, syrup, and cranberries in a medium size saucepan on medium heat and bring to a boil, stirring occasionally.

Gently simmer for10-12 minutes, stirring every couple of minutes.

Mixture will thicken and begin to set.

Allow to cool at room temperature, cover and place in the fridge for a day.

To make the bars:

Stir together flour, sugar, baking soda, salt, and oats in a large bowl.

In a separate bowl, whisk together honey and olive oil.

Pour wet ingredients over dry ingredients and combine with a pastry cutter. This will yield a crumbly consistency.

Reserve 1 cup of the above mixture, stir in chopped pecans and set aside.

Press the remainder of the mixture into an oiled 13"x 9" baking dish.

Bake: 350 for 20 minutes.

Remove from heat and pour 1 ¾ - 2 cups chilled cranberry filling evenly over dough.

Sprinkle the reserved crumble/ pecan mixture over the top of the cranberry filling.

Lightly press crumble into the filling with a fork. Take care not to burn your fingers on the hot dish!

Bake an additional 20-25 minutes until it has set and the edges are lightly browned.

Remove dish from oven and allow it to completely cool.

Once cool, cover the dish tightly with plastic wrap or foil.

Eat within 24 hours or refrigerate or freeze.

Options:

- Replace maple sugar with raw sugar.

- Replace honey with maple sugar or raw sugar, but the base layer won't hold together quite as well.

- If a glass baking dish is used, raise the oven rack one up from center.

- The cranberry sauce will keep for 2-3 weeks in the back of a 35 degree fridge, and also freezes well.

P. B. Carob Fudge**

This does a great job of satisfying that sweet tooth that hits in the middle of the afternoon. Having some in the freezer comes in handy also for a quick nutritious snack to go.

2-(2 ½) cups smooth peanut butter
½ cup honey

1 cup coarsely chopped walnuts
¾ cup finely ground oats
1 cup roasted carob powder
⅓ cup finely ground sesame seeds
¼ cup hemp seeds

Grease a 9"x9" baking dish with xv coconut oil.
Cut a piece of wax paper a little bigger than your dish, and set aside.
Mix together 2 cups of the peanut butter and the honey in a large bowl.
Separately mix remaining ingredients together and pour over PB and honey.
With your hands squish the ingredients together until well incorporated, adding more PB if needed to form a dense but moist dough. This will take a few minutes.
Scrape it into the baking dish, cover with wax paper and press hard on top to consolidate fudge and even out the top.
Cover and chill in fridge over night. Cut into squares and enjoy.
Keep refrigerated for up to a week, or freeze in individual squares.

Options:
- Omit hemp seeds and replace with an equal amount of ground oats.
- Pecans in place of walnuts are good.
- If you choose to omit the nuts all together, start with 1 ½ cups PB.
- Any nut butter you choose can be substituted for the peanut butter.
- Of course unsweetened cocoa powder can be substituted for the carob; initially reduce the cocoa powder to ¾ cup, adding in more to your taste.

Peanut Butter Ice Cream**

A cold, sweet, nutritionally dense treat that is simply delicious!

4 well spotted bananas
5-6 T peanut butter
½ tsp soft coconut oil (optional)
½ tsp vanilla extract

Peel and freeze bananas overnight.
Mix together the PB, oil, and vanilla. Set aside.
Set the freezer bag of bananas on the counter for 15-30 minutes until 30% thawed. (Err on the frozen side.)
Place in unplugged food processor and chop up with a fork to 1" pieces.
Process bananas until half whipped.
Break up any remaining chunks, add PB mixture and continue to whip until all smooth.
Eat as soft ice cream, or place in a sturdy freezer container and freeze for 1 hour or overnight, then eat.

Options:

- Chocolate: Place half the ice cream in a container and add 2 T cocoa powder or roasted carob powder to remaining half and whip until just blended. Lightly stir into PB ice cream and freeze. (Use ¼ cup powder for the whole batch, of course.)

Please note: Spotted bananas = creamy texture, unripe bananas = gooey texture. Whip only until smooth, as mixture will quickly melt beyond that point.

Pecan Pie Squares

Sweet, chewy, crunchy, rich flavor all packed in a little square!

Preheat oven to 350 degrees

1 cup spelt flour
⅓ cup fine ground quick oats
¼ tsp baking soda
3T maple sugar
¼ tsp whole salt
6T very soft soy margarine

½ cup maple syrup
½ tsp liquid lecithin
1 T olive oil
1 tsp vanilla extract
¾ tsp arrowroot powder
1cup + 2 T chopped pecans

Mix first 5 ingredients together, then cut in the soft margarine until a uniform consistency.
Firmly press into a 9"x9" baking dish greased with coconut oil.
Bake: 350 for 15-20 min, until puffy and set.
While that's baking, whisk together the remaining ingredients, adding the pecans at the last minute, just before spreading over the cooked base when it comes out of the oven.
Bake another 15-20 minutes until bubbly on the edges and lightly browned.
Cool completely to set properly before cutting into squares.

Please note: Take extra care to make sure the base is level before baking so the topping will be evenly distributed when added.

Pies

Everyday Pie Crust

1 cup spelt flour that's been kept in the freezer
¼ tsp whole salt
5 ½ T non-hydrogenated soy margarine, right out of the fridge
3-4 T ice cold water

Sprinkle half the flour in a 2 ½ quart bowl. Mix in salt.
Slice the margarine into the bowl and sprinkle the remaining flour on top.
Mix together with a pastry cutter until crumbly.
Add 3 T ice water and blend together with a fork adding the 4ᵗʰ T if too dry to form a soft ball. (Or more flour if a bit soggy will not harm the dough.)
Cut in two pieces for a two crust pie, or roll out the entire ball if you prefer a thicker single crust.

Please note: The ingredients need to be cold as stated to hold the crust together better, including getting it on the pie plate.
A well floured pastry cloth & roller cover makes this much easier. Also shaping and flattening the dough with floured fingers to about ⅓" thick before rolling out, ensures a more uniform shape.
Roll with equal pressure starting at the center rolling out to edge in a clock pattern: 12 to 6, 3 to 9, 10 to 4, and 8 to 2, repeating until a scant ⅛ " thick.
Gently fold the dough in half with flat side towards you.
Place the pie plate in front of crust, gently slide the crust to halfway point on plate, and carefully bring the top half of crust over other side.
Gently fit the crust into pie plate and cut the excess dough to approx 1" overhang.
If single crust pie, fold edge under and press top a bit in desired design.
If double crust, add filling, place top on in same fashion, fold top edge under bottom edge and press together. Slit top with sharp knife several times to release steam.
Extra dough left? Simply roll out and sprinkle with a 1: 6 ratio of cinnamon to raw or maple sugar.
Bake: 400 degrees for 3-6 minutes until lightly browned. Eat up as soon as cooled.

Gluten Free Pie Crust**

½ cup sorghum flour
¼ cup millet flour
2 T potato starch
¼ cup almond meal (or flour)
½ tsp arrowroot powder
3 T maple sugar
2 T brown rice flour

3-4 T light olive oil

Whisk all but the oil together well.

Cut in 3 T of oil. Mixture should be crumbly, but hold together when pressed along the side of the pie plate. Test a small area.

If it doesn't hold together, cut in ½ T more oil at a time until it holds together but is not gooey. (If you added too much oil, cut in a little more brown rice flour if you like a crunchy crust, a little sorghum if you prefer a softer crust.)

Press evenly and firmly along the pie plate sides and bottom. (This is geared towards a 9" deep-dish pie plate. If using a smaller one you may not need all of the mixture.)

Add the filling of any one-crust pie and bake as instructed.

Note: This recipe works well for single crust pies only.

Apple Pie & More

Apple pie, apple crisp. Which is better? There are more servings in apple crisp, but you really can't beat the first apple pie of the season.

Preheat oven to 400 degrees
4-5 cups peeled, cored apples sliced ¼"-⅓" thick. (Enough to fill a 9" deep dish pie plate, rounded on top.)
¼ cup spelt flour
1 tsp cinnamon
2 T light olive oil
⅓ cup honey
Every Day Pie Crust (page 98)

Place the apples in a large mixing bowl, stir in flour and cinnamon.
Wisk together the oil and honey, mix into the apples and set aside.
Make the Everyday Crust.
Add the filling.
Place pie in the preheated oven and reduce to 375 degrees.
Bake for 50-60 minutes until sharp fork inserted comes out easily and steam comes out slits.
Cool on cooling rack until set.

 Options:
- Cherry pie: Replace apples with 4 cups pitted sour cherries, reduce cinnamon to ½ tsp, increase honey to ½ cup.
- Strawberry rhubarb pie: Replace apples with 3 ½ cups diced ½" rhubarb, and 1 ½ cups diced strawberries.   Increase honey to ½ cup, omit cinnamon.
- Rhubarb pie: Replace apples with 4 cups diced (½") rhubarb, increase honey to ⅔ cups, reduce cinnamon to ½ tsp.
 - 3 ½ T arrowroot powder can be substituted for the spelt flour in any of the fruit pies.

Please note:

- Fresh fruit is recommended. Baking will take 10 or more minutes longer for frozen.
- With less fat in this crust, it is always better the first day, second day is still good.
- Except for the apple pie, the other fruit pies should bubble through slits a bit when done.

Tips:

-The amount of moisture in fruit varies. If a pie's filling isn't as thick as you like it, add/increase the amount of arrowroot powder by ½ T.
-Pie sweetness: These fruit pies have a lighter, fruitier flavor. If you like them sweeter, add 1 or 2 additional tablespoons of honey to what a recipe calls for.

Blueberry Pie

If you haven't had blueberry pie made with fresh blueberries, you haven't had blueberry pie yet!

Preheat oven to 425 degrees

4 cups fresh blueberries
3 ½ T arrowroot powder
⅓ cup honey
2 T light olive oil
Every Day Pie Crust (page 98)

Blend together all the filling ingredients and set aside.
Mix together the pie crust and split in two.
Roll out half the dough to ⅛" thick on a floured pastry cloth with a floured cloth covered rolling
  pin.
Gently fold in half, slide halfway over a 9" pie plate and unfold.
Gently form into pie plate, and cut the edge leaving a 1" overhang.
Roll out the second piece of pastry dough in the same manner.
Pour in the filling, add the top crust as you did the bottom, cutting the edge to match the bottom.
Fold both edges under and pinch together in your own design.
Make 3 or 4 slits an inch long in the top.
Place in the oven and reduce heat to 375 degrees.
Bake for 55-60 minutes until crust is lightly browned and the filling is bubbling.
Cool completely before serving.

Option: Replace arrowroot powder with 4-5 T spelt flour. Add ½ tsp cinnamon to mixture.

Peach Custard Pie*

A nice light pie for a warm summer evening. A breakfast favorite too.

Preheat oven to 400 degrees

1 ¼ cup spelt flour
⅛ tsp salt
¼ tsp baking powder
2 T maple sugar
3 ½ -4 T light olive oil

10-12 peaches, peeled, pitted, and sliced into ½" wedges
¼ cup honey
1 ¼ tsp cinnamon

1 ½ cups vanilla or plain soy yogurt
¾ tsp arrowroot powder
1 T apple cider vinegar

Mix together the flour, salt, baking powder and sugar.
Cut in 3 ½ T oil with a pastry cutter; flour should be fully incorporated and mixture crumbly. If too dry, mix in ½ T more. Press into a 9" deep-dish pie plate.
Prepare peaches and pour into pie crust.
Mix cinnamon with honey and drizzle evenly over peaches.
Bake: 400 for 15 minutes.
Thoroughly whisk together the yogurt, arrowroot powder then vinegar.
Remove pie from oven and pour enough over the peaches to reach ¼" below rim.
Set aluminum foil on oven rack (in case bubbles over), set pie on top and bake another 30-35 minutes until custard is set and tips are slightly browned.
Cool completely on cooling rack, cover and refrigerate overnight.

Options:
- Replace yogurt with 1 cup soy milk and reduce arrowroot powder to ½ tsp.
- For a peachier flavor reduce cinnamon to 1 tsp.

Gluten Free Option: Replace crumb crust with the Gluten Free Pie Crust (p. 99).

Pineapple Rhubarb Pie

Preheat oven to 400 degrees

3 ½ cups diced rhubarb
¾ cup crushed canned pineapple, well drained
⅛ tsp whole salt (optional)
4 T spelt flour
1 T arrowroot powder
⅔ cup honey
2 T light olive oil
Everyday Pie Crust (page 98)

Mix all ingredients together and set aside.
Make the crust, split in two for a bottom and top crust.
Place bottom crust in a 9" pie plate and pour in the filling.
Place on the top crust. Fold the 2 layers of crust and crimp together.
Make at least 4, ¾" slits on top.
Place in preheated 400 degree oven, reducing to 375.
Bake 45-55 minutes until crust is lightly browned on edges and juice bubbles through the slits.
Cool on cooling rack until set and cool.

Mmm... light and fruity.

Very Berry Pie

Preheat oven to 400 degrees

4 cups red or black raspberries
4 T spelt flour
⅔ cup honey, slightly warmed to thin
2 T light olive oil
Every Day Pie Crust (page 98)

Lightly mix the flour into the berries.
Blend together the oil and honey, fold into the berries and set aside.
Prepare the Every Day Pie Crust as described, placing the bottom crust in a 9" pie plate.
Pour the filling in and level off, roll and add the top crust as described.
Slice the top at least 3 times in your own decorative way.
Place the pie in the oven and reduce to 375 degrees.
Bake for 40-50 minutes until bubbles out the slits a bit and crust edge is lightly browned.
Set on cooling rack until cool and set.

Option: Use 4 ½ cups blackberries (aka thimbleberries) or elderberries or blueberries in place of raspberries and add 1 ½ T arrowroot powder with flour.

Chocolate Biscotti

Soft Oatmeal Cookies

Cookies

Molasses Crunchies

Chocolate Biscotti*

These are crispy without being hard, and will keep for weeks in a tightly sealed container or tin.

Preheat oven to 325 degrees and raise rack one up from the middle.

1 ½ cups spelt flour
1 tsp baking powder
¼ tsp baking soda
¼ tsp whole salt
3T ground flax seeds
½ tsp cream of tartar
½ cup cocoa powder

¼ cup light olive oil
1 tsp vanilla
¾ cup raw sugar
½ cup plain soy milk
1 tsp apple cider vinegar

Lightly grease 2 large, thick bottomed cookie sheets with xv coconut oil.
Separately mix dry and wet ingredients.
Gradually stir the dry into the wet. The dough will be quite stiff but moist.
Let it rest for 5-10 minutes.
Sprinkle a bit more flour as needed on dough and sides of bowl to scrape the dough out of the bowl.
With floured hands, form the dough to about 10" long.
Place in the middle of a cookie sheet and shape into a rectangle approx 3"x 12" and a scant 1" high.
Bake: 325 degrees for approx 25-30 minutes, until top springs right back when pressed in the center. If in doubt, bake a couple more minutes.
Remove from oven and reduce oven temp to 300 degrees.
Cool on rack for 15-20 minutes, until just slightly warm.
With two spatulas underneath, carefully transfer to a large cutting board.
Take a very thin, sharp, serrated knife (9"-10" long works well) & evenly press through to cut slices a little more than ½" thick. (You will have approx 14.) Wiping off knife between cuts is helpful.
Carefully transfer the pieces evenly between the 2 cookie sheets, leaving a minimum of 1½ - 2" between them.
Bake 1 sheet at a time at: 300 degrees for 11 minutes, until the side down is firm and dry.
Flip them over and bake another 9-10 minutes until dry to the touch.
Cool completely on a cooling rack before storing in a well sealed container.

Please note:
- Resist the temptation to bake them closer together as they don't bake up as well.
- These are perfect for mailing to someone for a treat as they keep for so long without refrigeration.

Gluten Free Option:
For Gluten Free Biscotti, replace spelt flour with the flours listed below. If more flour is needed for the proper consistency, use more chickpea flour. The taste and texture is so similar, no one ever notices any difference!

       ½ cup chickpea flour
       ¼ cup + 2 T potato starch
       ¼ cup + 2 T tapioca flour
       ¼ cup sorghum flour

Gluten Free Chocolate Chip Cookies**

Preheat oven: 350 degrees

Dry ingredients:
¾ cup chickpea flour
½ cup sorghum flour
¼ cup brown rice flour
1 ½ tsp arrowroot powder
½ tsp baking soda
2 T ground flax seeds
¼ tsp whole salt

Wet ingredients:
8 T soy margarine
⅓ cup maple sugar
2T maple syrup
¾ tsp vanilla
1-2 T soy milk

⅓ cup chopped walnuts
⅓ cup chocolate chips

Mix dry ingredients and set aside.
Cream wet ingredients well with electric mixer, then gradually beat in the dry until smooth, add-
   ing more soy milk as needed for a stiff but moist/sticky batter.
Stir in walnuts and chips.
Spoon onto a thick cookie sheet greased with ev coconut oil and squish down to approx ⅜" thick.
Bake: 350 for 8-12 minutes until center springs back.
Cool completely on cooling rack.

Option: Add ¼ tsp peppermint extract with wet ingredients.
Alternate flour ratio option: 1 cup chickpea, ½ cup sorghum, 2 T brown rice flour.

Molasses Crunchies

These are great for a sweet AND crunchy fix. Good dunkers too.

Oven temp: 350 degrees

2 ½ cups spelt flour
2 cups kamut flour
2 tsp whole salt
1 T ground ginger
1 tsp cinnamon
3 ½ tsp baking powder

2 tsp baking soda

1 cup soy margarine
2 cups unsulfured molasses

Mix together 1st 6 ingredients. Measure out baking soda in separate dish.
Melt margarine in a good sized pan with high sides.
Add molasses and bring to a simmer stirring constantly.
Remove from heat and stir in baking soda. (It will bubble up quite a bit.)
Gradually stir in the flour mixture, then let it sit for 10 minutes.
After 10 minutes, up to ½ cup flour may be gradually added to form a dense but soft dough.
Once the dough cools, cover and refrigerate for 3-10 hours.
Preheat oven to 350 degrees, raise oven rack one above middle.
Spoon out into 1" balls formed by rolling in the palms of your hands. Place at least 3" apart on a
    thick or air cushion cookie sheet greased with coconut oil or soy margarine.
Place a piece of wax paper over each ball, and flatten with the bottom of a large mug to approx ¼"
    thick, if not a bit thinner.
Bake: 350 for 8-12 minutes until center springs back when lightly pressed.
Remove from the oven, and let the cookies set for 2-4 minutes before transferring to a cooling
    rack. (Wait longer than that, they become part of the cookie sheet.)
Let cool completely and store in an airtight container for up to a week, or freeze.

Options:
- Use 1 cup unsulfured molasses and 1 cup blackstrap molasses for a more robust flavor.
- Bake the cookies a couple minutes less for a soft cookie.
- Use 1 ½ tsp salt for less of a salty/sweet flavor.

Molasses Raisin Cookies

A soft sweet cookie with a cup of tea will brighten any morning or afternoon!

Oven temp: 350 degrees

¾ cup light olive oil
¼ cup local honey
1 ¼ cups unsulfured molasses
½ cup plain soy milk
2 T of soaked chia seeds*

2 cups spelt flour (may need more)
2 cups kamut flour
3 T ground flax seeds
½ tsp whole salt
½ tsp baking soda
1 ½ tsp cinnamon
½ tsp ginger
¼ tsp nutmeg
¼ tsp clove
1-2 cups raisins

In a large bowl, whisk together the 5 wet ingredients.
In a separate bowl thoroughly mix together dry ingredients.
With a large spoon slowly and gradually stir the dry into the wet until just moistened.
Let it rest for 10 minutes. The dough should be quite thick, but still soft.
Gradually add more spelt flour as needed to acquire proper consistency.
Cover tightly and chill overnight, or at least 6 hours.
Scoop out approx ¼ cup of dough. On a floured surface, roll out to a ¼" thick disk.
Sprinkle a few raisins on half. Fold over and pinch closed. Repeat process with remaining dough.
Place on a thick, greased cookie sheet 2" apart.
Bake: 350 degrees for 6-10 minutes until center of cookie springs back when pressed lightly.
Cool completely on cooling rack before storing in an airtight container for up to a week.

*Soaked chia seeds: Mix ½ cup water with 1 T chia seeds in a cup container. Stir up a couple times in the 1st hour then store covered in the fridge overnight. Use up any extra in 1-2 days in other recipes or just eat them as is.

Option: Omit raisins, form cookie dough into 3" x ½" disks. Bake as above.

Soft Oatmeal Cookies*

These are very popular with everyone, but differing opinions on how many nuts and raisins to include are reflected in the ranges below.

Preheat oven to 350 degrees

Dry ingredients:

1 cup spelt flour
1 cup kamut flour
1 tsp baking soda
½ tsp whole salt
¼ cup ground flax seeds
2 ½ cups finely chopped old fashioned oats

Wet ingredients:

1 cup almond milk
½ tsp apple cider vinegar
2 T chia seed/water mix*
2 tsp vanilla extract
1 cup coconut oil, warmed to liquefy
½ cup honey
½ cup maple sugar

½-¾ cup walnuts or pecans, chopped
½-¾ cup raisins

Stir together the dry ingredients.
Separately stir together the 7 wet ingredients in a large bowl.
Gradually mix the dry into the wet until just moistened.
Fold in the nuts and raisins.
Drop large spoonfuls onto a thick bottomed cookie sheet oiled with coconut oil.
Shape into 2 ½" x ½" thick rounds, 1 ½"-2" apart.
Bake: 350 degrees for 8-10 minutes, until cookie springs back when lightly pressed in the center.
Immediately remove from sheet and cool on cooling rack.
Store in an airtight container for 2-3 days or freeze whatever isn't gobbled right up!

*Chia seed mix: Stir together ½ cup water with 1 T chia seeds. Stir occasionally for first hour then cover and set in fridge for 12-24 hours. Measure out what is needed for recipe. The rest can be thrown into a shake, hot cereal, or whatever you like for an added nutritional boost. Soaking overnight gives the seeds a chance to gel more thoroughly before using.

Gluten Free Option: Replace spelt and kamut flour with: 1 cup buckwheat flour, ½ cup brown rice flour, ¼ cup almond flour, ¼ cup sorghum flour and ¼ tsp xanthan gum. Mix together well with a small whisk before adding the remaining ingredients as stated above.

Apple Cinnamon Air Freshener "Cookies"

These are made out of food, but I don't recommend eating them!
Set them in a dish, or cut a ¼" hole in them before drying and hang on a Christmas tree or anywhere you want the sweet smell of cinnamon. Some we made over 10 years ago still have a faint scent.

1 cup ground cinnamon
¾ cup applesauce

Mix together, adding more of either to produce a soft but firm dough.
Roll out to a ¼" thickness, using extra cinnamon so it doesn't stick.
Cut into shapes, re-rolling any scraps. The easiest way to make the hole; remove the eraser from a pencil to punch one hole out at a time, using a toothpick to remove the dough each time.
Dehydrate until pieces are hard and dry. (Can also dry in the oven at 150 degrees for 2-3 hours depending on the thickness.) Cool completely.

These are fun to make and to give away!

Easy Salsa Casserole

Zesty Pesto

Main Dishes

Marinated Grilled Veggies

Beans and Greens**

This is one of the favorites. Easy, but oh so satisfying!

2 T xv olive oil
2 large cloves garlic, chopped fine (2-3 T)

1-1 ½ # escarole, cleaned and chopped into 2"-3" pieces (1 large head)

1 veggie bouillon cube mixed with 1 cup hot escarole water
2 cups drained navy pea beans

1-2 T arrowroot powder mixed with ¼ cup room temperature water

Heat a 12", high-sided cast iron pan on medium low. Sauté garlic in oil for a minute.
Blanch escarole in a big pot of salted boiling water (4-5 quarts to 1 tsp salt) for just a couple min-
    utes until just tender. Reserve a couple cups liquid, drain and add to garlic.
Mix for a minute then stir in bouillon and beans. Cover and simmer on low for 5 minutes. (If too
    much liquid has evaporated, add another ½ cup or more as needed.)
Shake together 1 T arrowroot and ¼ cup water. Add and stir until thickens and begins to bubble.
    Repeat if like a thicker mix.
Serve with whole grain bread or over long grain brown rice.*

Options: Replace escarole with ½-¾ # kale; center rib removed, cut in 2"-3" pieces (approx 8 cups
    lightly packed). Blanch for 5-7 minutes until just tender. 1-1 ½ # swiss chard works well too,
    or half chard and half kale. (Be sure to blanch greens until tender, otherwise they will be tough
    and stringy.)
Please note: For a juicier mix, start with 1 ½ cups escarole water, and up to 3 T arrowroot powder
    as needed. Can also add up to 3 cups beans depending on your taste.

*Long grain brown rice: 1 ½ rounded cups long grain brown rice, 3 cups water, 1 veggie bouillon
    cube. Bring to a simmer, reduce heat to very low, cover and cook 40 minutes. Remove from
    heat and keep covered 10-15 more minutes. Fluff and serve.

Escarole

Burrito Shells

These are especially delicious fresh out of the pan, but out of the freezer are a surprisingly close
   second! With a salad, makes a nice light dinner.

4 cups spelt flour	½ cup xv olive oil
1 cup unbleached flour	
2 tsp whole salt	1 ½ cups boiling water

Lightly oil a cookie sheet and set aside. Stir together flours and salt.

Blend in oil with a pastry cutter until a dry/ crumbly texture.

Pour in the boiling water and mix with a fork until forms a ball. (May need a bit more water.)

Knead gently and slowly for 2-3 minutes, then pull off pieces of dough a little bigger than a golf
   ball, knead just a bit, and place on a lightly oiled cookie sheet a few inches from the edges.
   (Rows of three work out well.)

Cover with a smooth damp towel and let set for 7-9 hours.

Preheat a 15" cast iron fry pan on a little higher than medium heat.   (Approx 5 minutes.)

With the rest of the dough covered, with floured fingers, flatten one piece of dough until ⅓" thick.
   Then roll out on floured surface with floured rolling pin to ⅟₃₂" thick. (For rolling instructions
   look under "Pie Crust" in "Tips Worth Reading" p. 167.)

With lightly floured hands, lift up from underneath, gently pass from one hand to the other to
   loosen excess flour and carefully flip onto the dry pre-heated pan.

In a few seconds small bubbles will begin to form. Carefully flip over with an extra thin heat-
   resistant non-metalic spatula. Cook for 30 seconds.

Flip over for 30 more seconds, remove from pan and place under a damp towel while the rest are
   cooked.

There should be a few medium brown spots on the cooked shells. If spots are black lower the
   temperature a bit, if no spots, raise it a bit.

Fill with your favorite goodies, e.g., beans, rice, salsa, lettuce, avocado.

Please note: Extras freeze well. Place in a 2 gallon freezer bag with wax paper between each, setting on a flat surface such as a large dinner plate to freeze. To thaw, place a shell under a damp
   dish towel for 5-7 minutes. Yield: approx fifteen 10"-12" shells.

Burrito Filling

Add some beans, lettuce, salsa, and cooked brown rice; wrap up in a burrito shell, or scoop into a bowl.   Good with black beans, pintos, or refried beans.

2 T xv olive oil
1 small onion (approx ⅓ cup)
1 large clove garlic (1 T), chopped fine
1 pkg (12 oz) Yves veggie ground
1 tsp Braggs liquid aminos
½ tsp cumin
1/16 tsp cayenne pepper
¼ tsp black pepper

2 cups canned tomatoes

Sauté on low in order listed up to the tomatoes, stirring frequently for a couple minutes. Stir in tomatoes. Simmer on low for 5-10 minutes for flavors to meld together.

Also goes nicely with cornbread.

Calzones & Pizza

The best part of vegan calzones is they stay moist and juicy inside.

Preheat oven to 400 degrees. Place pizza stone on oven rack lowered to bottom level.

Dough:

4 cups lukewarm water

4 T yeast

4 T honey

4 T granular lecithin

½-⅔ cup xv olive oil

4 tsp whole salt

4 tsp garlic powder

11-12 cups spelt flour

Filling/ Topping:

14-18 oz. portabella mushrooms, sliced

2-3 cups pizza sauce (16-24 oz.)

1 large sweet white onion, diced

1 large sweet pepper, diced (green, red)

Any LIGHTLY sautéed bite sized veggies of your choice

Garlic powder, basil, oregano, whole salt, xvoo

Stir together dough ingredients respectively, adding just enough flour to form into a ball.
Knead slowly and gently for 5-10 minutes until dough springs back.
Oil your mixing bowl, flip dough over in it to oil all sides, leaving smooth side up.
Cover with a warm damp towel and set aside for 30-40 minutes.

While dough is rising, slice up the mushrooms, and dice onions and peppers in ½" pieces.

For calzones:
Gently push down dough, and divide into 12 equal pieces, keeping all but the piece you are using under the damp towel.
With oiled hands, form into a round or square flattened to approx ¼" thick.
On half of the piece add 1T or so of sauce, then roughly 2T of filling ingredients.
Sprinkle with herbs, salt, and a drizzle of xvoo. (Keep the filling at least ½" from edges.)
Fold other half over, pinching the edges tightly closed.
Set on floured area until you have at least 4.
Place on preheated pizza stone.
Bake: 400 for 12-15 minutes until lightly browned and bottom crispy.

Cool on cooling rack. Repeat with remaining dough.
Store any leftovers in bag in fridge to eat within 24hrs.

For pizza:
Split dough into two pieces to make two 12"-14" pizzas.
Spread dough partially with oiled fingers, then press to desired size and thickness on the pizza stone, taking care not to burn your fingers (¼"-⅜" thick works well).
Sprinkle with garlic powder, sauce, drizzle of oil, herbs, salt, toppings, and a bit more sauce.
As with the calzones, remember to be more liberal with the oil and salt to replace some of the fat and salt cheese adds to pizza.
Bake at the same temp and amount of time as the calzones.
Eat up, or keep in fridge for 24 hours, or freeze.

Options: Add fresh minced garlic. Add shredded vegan cheese

Creamy Curried Beans & Rice*

7 T xv olive oil
2-3 T onion, chopped
1 small clove garlic, chopped fine

2 tsp lecithin, granular or liquid
2 tsp whole salt
6 T spelt flour
¼ tsp black pepper
1 -1 ½ T curry powder

3 cups plain soy milk

1 T fresh lemon juice
1 ½ cups navy pea beans, warmed and drained

4 cups just cooked brown rice (2 cups dry)

In a medium size pan, slightly sauté first 3 ingredients for a couple minutes.
Stir in next 5 ingredients until it bubbles.
Slowly pour the soy milk in while whisking, continuing until mixture thickens and bubbles.
Stir in the lemon juice and beans and adjust the curry to taste.
Divide the rice into 4 bowls, pour the sauce and beans over the rice.
Add a green salad full of fresh raw veggies and you have a quick dinner.
The sauce also freezes well for future meals, and is good with either spicy or sweet curry powder.

Option: Omit flour, reserve ½ cup soy milk. When the cream sauce comes to a simmer, shake together ¼ cup soy milk with 3 T arrowroot powder. Stir until comes back to a simmer. If you like a thicker sauce, shake up the remaining ¼ cup soy milk with 1 T more arrowroot powder and stir in. If thick enough at first, just add in the last ¼ cup milk.

Easy Salsa Casserole**

The importance of a few meals that involve mixing everything in one dish and cooking it cannot be overstated!

Preheat oven to 375 degrees

2 cups medium salsa

1 ½ cups black beans, drained

1 cup reserved bean juice

1 ¼ cups fresh corn kernels

1 cup long grain brown rice, uncooked

1 ¾ cups canned tomatoes, cut up in jar before measuring

½ veggie bouillon cube

¾ tsp basil

½ tsp whole salt

½ tsp cumin

¼ tsp black pepper (optional)

Add all the ingredients in a medium casserole dish that will have an inch at the top for expansion. Cover with aluminum foil VERY TIGHTLY.

Bake: 375 degrees for approx 1 hour 45 minutes, until rice is moist and fluffy.

Recover, let set on cooling rack for 10-15 minutes and serve.

Great by itself, even better with a green salad and cornbread.

Please note:
- If using canned beans that have salt in them, omit the ¼ tsp salt.
- Should you be short on bean juice, water or tomatoes can be used to bring amount up to 1 cup.

Marinated Grilled Veggies**

This is easily adapted to any fresh veggies you prefer. On a hot muggy night, what more could you want? Well, maybe some Peanut Butter Ice Cream for dessert.

Marinade:

½ cup light olive oil
Juice of ½ a large lemon (approx 2 T)
2 large cloves garlic, minced (approx 2 T)
⅛-¼ tsp cayenne pepper
1 ¼ tsp whole salt
½ tsp fresh ground black pepper
7 large basil leaves chopped fine (approx 3 T fresh, or 1 T dry)
½-1 T fresh oregano chopped fine (or 1 tsp dry)

10 plus cups fresh veggies, such as:
    3 large portabella mushrooms, stemmed and cut in thirds, then cut crosswise in ⅓" slices
    1 ½ cups sugar snap peas, strings removed. (Snap off the tips and pull towards the center.)
    3 small 7" long zucchini, ends removed and sliced ¼" thick
    2 sweet red peppers, hulled and cut into 1" pieces or ½" slices
    1 medium-large white sweet or yellow cooking onion (tough outer layers removed), sliced in
        ¼"-⅓" thick disks and separated into circles (approx 1 ½ cups).

1 pound extra firm tofu, drained, patted dry, and cut into ¾" cubes. Spread out in one layer on
    a non-fuzzy towel, place another towel over it and press down lightly for the extra moisture to
    absorb into the towels. Leave for 20-30 minutes.

Mix the marinade together and set aside.
Mix the prepared veggies and tofu in a large bowl and fold in the marinade until veggies are well
    coated. Let sit for 30-40 minutes stirring up occasionally.
Place a large high sided grill basket on the preheated grill set at medium high.

Set the veggies in a single but cozy layer, flipping over every few minutes until all sides are grilled
   and the veggies are crisp-tender.
Closing the lid between stirrings will shorten the cooking time to approx 20 minutes.
Pour in a bowl and serve.

Options:
- De-stem then slice mushrooms into 2 discs, the zucchini lengthwise ⅜" thick, and the peppers in
   quarters. Place all prepared veggies on cookie sheets, brush with marinade, flip over and repeat.
   Grill as above, with the option to cook the larger pieces right on the grill.
- Reserve 1-2 T of marinade to brush on a couple yams or baking potatoes that have been sliced
   lengthwise. Wrap them in foil, and bake on the edges of the grill not being used by the veggie
   basket. Grill 10-15 minutes cut side up, then flip and cook another 10-15 minutes until soft.
   (When punctured with a fork, it slides out easily.) If all the marinade is needed, just brush them
   with olive oil, and sprinkle with salt, pepper, and lots of garlic powder. Simply delicious!

Red Lentil Round**

This makes 6-8 generous pie-shaped servings.
Great hot topped with spaghetti sauce, in a sandwich the next day, or just by itself.
It freezes well too.

Preheat oven to 350 degrees

Recipe #1
4 cups water
2 cups red lentils
¼ cup teff
1 small bay leaf

3 T xv olive oil
1 ½ T garlic, minced
1 ½ cups onions, chopped
½ # extra firm tofu, crumbled
1 ½ tsp thyme
½ tsp basil
¼ tsp oregano

3 T ground flax seeds
½ cup whole grain bread crumbs
½ cup finely ground oats
2 ½ tsp whole salt
½ tsp black pepper

2-3 T fresh lemon juice
3 T fresh Italian parsley, chopped fine

Recipe #2 (gluten free)
5 cups water
2 ½ cups red lentils
¾ cup teff
1 small bay leaf

¼ cup xv olive oil
2 T garlic, minced
2 cups white or yellow onions, chopped
1 ½ tsp thyme
½ tsp basil
¼ tsp savory

2 T ground flax seeds
⅓ cup fine ground oats (or oat flour)
1 T whole salt
¾ tsp black pepper
1 ½ tsp arrowroot powder

¼ cup fresh lemon juice
3-4 T parsley, chopped fine

Bring the first group of ingredients to a low simmer, covered.

Cook until the lentils are soft. Remove bay leaf.

In a separate pan, sauté on low the 2nd group of ingredients, stirring frequently until the onions are soft.

In a large bowl mix the 3rd group of ingredients together.

Once the first 2 mixtures have cooled to warm, mix all the ingredients together, adding the lemon juice and parsley last.

Spread evenly into a lightly oiled 10" spring form pan.

Bake: 350 degrees for 50-60 minutes until the edge is lightly browned and the center is firm.

Set on cooling rack for a minimum of 30 minutes before cutting into. It will set more as it cools.

This is even better after the flavors meld together overnight.

Option:
- In recipe #1, drain and freeze tofu ahead, thaw out the day you need it. Squeeze any remaining water out and crumble. Continue as above. (This will produce a firmer round.)
- In recipe #2, you can also reduce teff to ½ cup and add ½ cup of chickpea flour.
- In recipe #2, oregano can be substituted for the savory.

Spicy Veggie Pockets

Aka samosas or dumplings; delicious by any name!

Pocket dough:
1 ½ cup unbleached flour
1 ¼ tsp whole salt
½-¾ cup water

3 T light olive oil

Filling:
2 T light olive oil
1 ½ T garlic, chopped fine
1 ¾ cups onion, chopped fine
4 tsp hot curry powder
1 tsp sweet curry powder

2 ½-3 cups russet potatoes, peeled and diced (¼")
1 ½ cups carrots, diced fine
1 ½ cups fresh or frozen peas
¾ tsp whole salt
½ tsp black pepper

½ veggie bouillon cube mixed with:
¾ cup boiling water

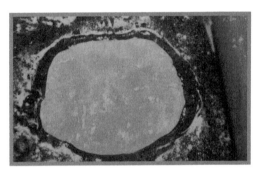

Pocket dough:
Mix flour and salt together. Cut in the oil with a pastry cutter. (Pour the oil over the flour and salt mixture and in a chopping motion mix the oil in until a crumbly consistency.)
With a fork, stir in just enough of the water to form a soft ball of dough.
Slowly and gently knead until a nice, smooth ball forms.
Return to mixing bowl and cover with a damp towel for 30-40 minutes (2 hours maximum).
Make the filling while the dough rests.

Filling:
Gently sauté onion, garlic and curry powders in oil until onion is soft, stirring occasionally.
Add other veggies, salt and pepper. Mix well.
Stir and simmer for a minute then add veggie bouillon/water mixture.
Bring to a low simmer and cover, simmering until veggies are just a little crisp-tender, stirring every couple minutes. Remove from heat and uncover to cool.

Making pockets:

Divide dough into eighteen equal pieces; return to the bowl and cover, taking one piece out at a time.

With floured hands, gently form a piece into a small round disk ¼" thick, then place on a lightly floured counter and roll out with a rolling pin to a very thin (1⁄32 inch or less) circle, 4 ½"-5" in diameter. (Yes, the dough will stretch to this thickness and width.)

Once rolled out, slice the circle in half and *lightly* moisten half of the edges with a pastry brush dipped in water. Take one piece and place 1-1 ½ T veggie mix on the moistened half, keeping edges clear. Fold over the other side to make a semicircle and press edges together with floured fingers to make a closed pocket.

Repeat process with remaining dough, placing finished pockets on a floured surface until you have 6-7 to bake or 4-5 to fry.

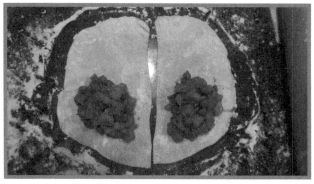

*See more photos
on the next page.*

Cooking Options:

- Baked (crunchy): Bake: 400 degrees on oiled cookie sheet 1-2" apart for 7 minutes until medium brown on the bottom. Flip over and bake 6-7 additional minutes until medium brown on edges and bottom. Place on a paper towel covered plate and serve hot.

- Fried (crispy): Heat a 12" heavy bottom or cast-iron skillet to medium high. Add peanut oil to a level of ½". Heat oil and watch carefully to avoid smoking. (If oil is too cool, too much oil will absorb into the pockets. Too hot, will splatter oil everywhere and burn the pockets.) Carefully slide 4-5 pockets into the oil, leaving 1-2" between them. Gently turn over with tongs when they are medium brown on the bottom (1-2 minutes depending on the temperature of the oil). When both sides are brown, place on 2 layers of paper towels to absorb extra oil. Serve hot.

Please note: These warm up well and are very good cold too for food on the go. The fried ones are good fresh, as well as the baked, but the baked ones stay nicer for future leftovers.

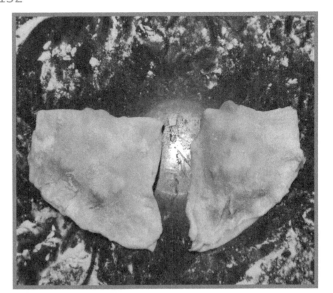

Zesty Pesto**

This is a great way to get more raw greens, and the aftertaste is very nice.
A spoonful in a bowl of potato or minestrone soup is wonderful!

½ cup xv olive oil
2 cups fresh basil leaves, well packed
1 cup fresh Italian parsley, well packed
½ tsp whole salt
⅔ cup pine nuts
2 large cloves garlic, chopped (2 T)

Blend all in a food processor until very smooth.
Mix into pasta or brown rice.
Goes well with a salad topped with a few beans, such as black, pinto, or chic peas.
Blanched, chilled green beans are a very good accompaniment too.

Option: Include 2-3 T well-drained navy pea beans for a little milder flavor and an extra bit of
    protein.

Slow Cooked "Baked" Beans

Side Dishes

Sweet Potato Casserole

Creamy Escalloped Potatoes

Anything with potatoes and garlic that's creamy just screams comfort food!
A good recipe for a dish to pass.

Preheat oven to 350 degrees

4 T vegan margarine
1 cup xv or light olive oil
3 ½ tsp whole salt
2 T granular lecithin
1 tsp fresh ground black pepper
1 clove garlic, minced (1T)

1 cup spelt flour
8 cups plain soy milk
3 cups plain rice milk

3-4 medium size onions
5-6 # white potatoes

In a large pot bring first 6 ingredients to a low simmer, stirring with a whisk.
Gradually stir in the flour.
When begins to bubble, gradually pour in the soy milk and rice milk stirring slowly but constantly.
Stir over medium heat until mixture thickens a bit and bubbles. Turn off heat and set aside.
Slice onions and potatoes ¼" thick, discarding the potato ends.
Lightly oil a 10" x 15" high-sided casserole dish. Pour in enough sauce to cover bottom ¼".
Layer potatoes, overlapping 50%, to cover the bottom. Break up the onions into ringlets.
Spread enough over the potatoes for the ringlets to overlap a bit.
Pour on enough sauce to cover onions. Continue the process until filled to ¾" from the top, making sure the last layer is generously covered with sauce.
Bake: 350 degrees, uncovered for 1 ½ - 2 ½ hours, depending on how many layers you ended up with. (It's generally around 2 hours.)
When a serving fork comes out of the potatoes easily in the center they are done.
Set on a cooling rack, place a flat sheet of foil over the top and let it set for approx 30 minutes before serving. (It will thicken up as it cools, but have bowls on hand to serve in.)

Please note:
- This expands as it cooks. Placing a large piece of foil under the dish in the oven is good insurance in case it bubbles over.
(Continued)

Creamy Escalloped Potatoes (Continued)

- Whatever ingredients you have left, toss them in a bowl and cover them with sauce and bake. (FYI- the smaller amount will cook quicker.)
- A food processor makes quick work of the slicing, and a ¼" blade often comes with it.
- Why rice milk too? It thins the sauce out a bit and gives it a lighter flavor. (If too much is used it doesn't thicken well.)

Options:
- Onions are optional, but add a lot of flavor.
- Replacing the rice milk with 3 more cups soy milk is an option.

Quick Escalloped Potatoes**

These take half as long to cook and are light, creamy, and full of flavor.

Preheat oven: 400 degrees

2 ¼ - 2 ½ # white potatoes (6-7 cups)
1 T olive oil
1¾ cup water
½ cup white or yellow onion, chopped fine
½ large clove garlic, chopped fine (½ T)

Sauce:
2 T olive oil
1 tsp liquid lecithin
1 ¾-2 T arrowroot powder
¼ tsp black pepper
1 ½ tsp whole salt
1 ¼ cup plain soy milk

1-2 T parsley, chopped fine

In a lightly oiled 10" x 10" baking dish, stir together the potato mixture.
Cover VERY TIGHTLY with aluminum foil.
Bake: 400 for 20 minutes. While cooking, whisk together the sauce in order listed.
Remove potatoes from oven and mix in the sauce. Tightly seal again and bake another 20 minutes.
Remove from oven, add parsley, stir up well. Bake for 10-20 minutes more until potatoes are done.
Remove from oven, leave covered, and let set 20-30 minutes before serving.

Pickled Beets**

These are great for a summer treat, in winter when you need a taste of summer, and a great way to use an over abundance of beets in the fall. So much fresher and tastier than the store bought ones!

4 cups water
1 cup honey
½ cup apple cider vinegar
1 peck of beets (8 quarts)

Bring a large pot of water to a boil; enough to cover beets by several inches.
While waiting to boil, scrub the beets clean.
Place in boiling water, bring back to a simmer and cook until beets are almost tender (when a slender serving fork easily pierces through the center of the beet).
While beets are cooking, place the 4 cups water, honey and vinegar in a pot and bring to a boil.
Simmer on low for at least a couple minutes. Cover and turn off heat.
Place 7 quart jars upside down in a hot water bath canner, adding enough water to cover the jars halfway up. Cover, bring to a boil and simmer for at least 2 minutes. Leave on low.
In a smaller covered pot, add the lids and rings. Cover with 1-2" water, bring to a boil for 1-2 minutes. Cover and turn off burner.
When beets are cooked, spread out on a cookie sheet to cool.
Bring lids, jars, and syrup back to a simmer.
When beets cool just enough for you to handle them, peel and slice them ¼"- ⅓" thick and place in a bowl.
Gently pack the sterilized jars with beets, pour the syrup to ¼"- ½" from the top. Wipe the top with a clean, damp paper towel. Securely add hot lid and ring, and set 2" apart on a thick towel upside down for 5-7 minutes.
Right the jars and leave undisturbed for 24 hours. Check to see if all jars sealed, clean off the jars and store in the fridge.
If you wish to store outside the fridge, process in a hot water bath canner for 30 minutes then place upright on towel as above. Check to make sure tops sealed, wipe jars clean and store in cool, dark, dry place. Leave beets for at least 2 weeks before opening to give them a chance to start pickling. Eat unsealed jars first of course!

Option: A 2"-3" stick of cinnamon may be added while the syrup is simmering.

Saucy Baked Cauliflower

This is a nice side dish, and a leftover bowl of it makes a quick lunch.

Preheat oven to 350 degrees
1 medium cauliflower, cut into flowerettes, extra stems discarded. (approx 6 cups)
2 T xv olive oil
1 cup water

½ cup fresh whole grain bread crumbs
¼ cup nutritional yeast flakes
¼ tsp oregano
¾ tsp basil
1 tsp whole salt
2 T xv olive oil

Mix the first 3 ingredients together in a large casserole dish.
Bake covered at 350 degrees for 30-40 minutes until cauliflower is still crisp but almost done.
Blend together the breadcrumb mix and stir into the crisp-tender cauliflower thoroughly.
Bake another 10- 15 minutes until cauliflower is just cooked, stir up again and serve.

Note: Err on the el dente side. Over cooked cauliflower is a whole different taste.

Gluten Free Option: Omit bread crumbs for a gluten free dish.

Savory Potatoes**

A welcome change from a regular baked potato!

Preheat oven: 375 degrees
⅓ cup xv olive oil
1 ½ tsp garlic powder
½ tsp whole salt
1 ¾ tsp paprika

1 tsp thyme
½ tsp black or white pepper

5-7 white potatoes or 3-4 russet potatoes

Whisk together all ingredients (except the potatoes) for the marinade.
Slice the potatoes in ¾" wedges and place skin side down on a cookie sheet.
Brush the cut sides with marinade.
Bake: 375 for 35-40 minutes until the potatoes are done, and a fork comes out easily.

Option: Replace paprika and thyme with 1 ½ tsp basil, ½ tsp oregano.

Slow Cooked "Baked" Beans**

Cook this in your slow cooker for a very moist, sweet, savory baked bean flavor.

¾ cup maple syrup
⅓ cup unsulfured molasses
⅓ cup honey
4 tsp dry mustard
4 tsp dry ginger
2 tsp cinnamon

2 tsp whole salt
1 cup fresh bean juice
¾ cup white sweet onion, chopped fine

11 cups cooked, drained navy pea beans (or seven 15.5 oz cans)

In a large slow cooker, mix together all but the beans, then stir in the beans.
Cover and cook on low for 6-8 hours, until liquid has absorbed to your preferred consistency.
Stir every couple hours.
If canned beans are used, rinse well and use water instead of bean juice.
Navy pea beans are my first choice, but great northern beans work well also.

Sweet Potato Casserole**

A light, pleasantly sweet dish. If you need a reason to eat more sweet potatoes, this is a good one!
Preheat oven to 350 degrees

1 ½ T honey
⅛ tsp whole salt
1 ¼ tsp vanilla
¾ tsp arrowroot powder
⅓ cup plain soy milk
4 cups yams (or sweet potatoes);
    baked, peeled, and mashed

3 T fine ground oats (or oat flour)
¼ cup quick oats
¾ cup chopped pecans
3 T light olive oil
⅓ cup maple sugar

Stir together first 6 ingredients respectively, then whip until creamy with an electric mixer.
Pour into an oiled 9" x 9" baking dish and level off.
In a separate bowl mix together the topping and sprinkle evenly over the sweet potato mix.
Bake: 350 for 35-45 minutes until heated through and just a touch browned on top.
Let set for 5-10 minutes and serve. Good cold too for lunches!

Options: Replace soy milk with strained almond milk, honey with maple syrup, and maple sugar with maple syrup. If maple syrup is used in the topping, blend with the oil before mixing with remaining ingredients. The result is more crusty than crumbly. Also very good cold for lunches!

Cranberry sauce

Chickpea Hummus and More

Sauces, Spreads, Dips and Drinks

Maple Cranberry Sauce**

Once you've tried fresh cranberry sauce without all the refined sugar there's no going back!

¾ cup water
1 cup maple syrup
3 cups fresh cranberries

Bring the water and syrup to a boil, being careful not to boil over.
Stir in the cranberries, bring back to a medium simmer and cook for 10-12 minutes, stirring every couple minutes until thickens.
A wooden spoon used for stirring, held horizontally over the pot should drop two drops at a time when done.
Immediately pour into a heat-proof container.
Cool completely and store covered in the fridge. (A thicker skin may form on top. This is normal.)
Freezes well.

Note: If frozen in 2 cup amounts, you're all set to make a batch of cranberry bars any time of year!

Elderberry Syrup**

This recipe has a fresher berry flavor and sweetness than other syrups I have tried.

5 cups elderberries, stemmed and rinsed (approx 1 ⅔ #)
2 cups water
1 cup local honey

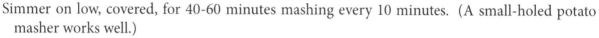

Bring berries and water to a simmer.

Simmer on low, covered, for 40-60 minutes mashing every 10 minutes. (A small-holed potato masher works well.)

Berries are ready when the seeds have floated to the surface & there are just a few skins still intact.

Place a fine mesh colander over a second pan and pour in the berry mix. (Cheese cloth may be placed over colander if the holes are too large.) Let drip for 10-15 minutes, pressing lightly at the end to express the last of the juice taking care not to push seeds through.

This will yield approx 3 cups juice.

Set aside the pulp.

Stir the honey into the juice until dissolved.

(I drink one tablespoon a day during the winter months; a tablespoon three times a day if I have a sore throat or cold.)

Good on pancakes, too!

Option 1: Place liquid in sterilized jars and store in the fridge for up to a month.

Option 2:
Simmer on low for 3-5 minutes. (It will become a little more syrupy.)

Pour into 1 cup sterilized canning jars to ¼" from top. Attach sterilized lids and rings, seal tightly.

Place upside down on a towel on your counter for 7 minutes.

Carefully right the jars and leave for 24 hours. Be sure all have sealed.

Wash off and store in a cool, dark, dry place for up to a year.

This is the old fashioned way I have used for decades with great success.

Please be aware it is now recommended to process in a water bath canner for 10 minutes before resting for 24 hours and storing.

Creamy Horseradish Spread**

Add a little extra zing to your next sandwich and veggies!

¼ cup vegan mayonnaise
5 tsp lightly drained horseradish sauce
¼ tsp whole salt
⅛ tsp white pepper
½ tsp fresh parsley, chopped fine (optional)
¼ tsp xanthan gum powder

Whisk all together until very creamy.
Spread on your favorite sandwich, or use as a dip for raw veggies.
Spread over slices of fresh in season tomatoes and cucumbers, makes eating healthy truly joyous!

Options: If you like a thicker spread, store in the fridge 6-8 hours before using, or add a bit more
xanthan gum.

Fresh Horseradish Sauce**

All you need are fresh roots and apple cider vinegar.

Dig up the roots of the horseradish plants; the larger the root, the hotter the sauce.

Also processing immediately after digging will produce the hottest sauce the roots are capable of, as they lose their potency within 2-3 hours after digging.

Scrub the roots clean, cut into 1" pieces and place in a large food processor, preferably plugged in outside. Process until very small bits.

Through the feeder tube pour enough vinegar to produce a creamy mixture, then add a little more to get a consistency a little more liquefied than what you buy in the store, as the horseradish will absorb more vinegar as it sits in your fridge the first couple days.

KEEP YOUR FACE WAY AWAY WHEN YOU OPEN THE LID! The fumes cause an extreme burning sensation best avoided!

When the sauce is ready, immediately spoon into rubber sealed jars, leaving at least ½" space for expansion. (Empty jelly jars or one cup canning jars work well.)

This sauce will keep in the fridge for several months.

If you wish to freeze some after a couple days, be sure there is still ample space for expansion.

Sealing them tightly and also placing them in a freezer bag will keep them for 2-3 years in a 0 degree, manual defrost freezer.

Quince Jam**

There is no smell more wonderful than quince simmering on the stove. I can't describe it to you, because there is no comparison!

3 ¼ # washed and cored quince fruit, good skin left on
8 cups water
½ tsp fresh lemon juice (optional)

4 cups of above when cooked
2 T fresh lemon juice
1 T calcium water mixture (1/4 tsp calcium powder mixed with 1/4 cup water)

1 T pectin powder
1 cup honey

Have hot, sterilized 8 oz jelly jars, lids, and rings ready.
Chop quince into ⅛"-¼" pieces in a food processor.
Bring water, ½ tsp lemon juice, and quince to a low simmer, uncovered.
Stir occasionally, simmering until fruit just barely becomes soft. Remove from heat.
In a small bowl mix the pectin powder thoroughly into the honey and set aside.
Measure 4 cups of fruit mixture and place in a medium size, thick bottomed sauce pan.
Bring back to a simmer and stir in the 2 T lemon juice and calcium water.
Bring to a simmer again and stir in the honey/pectin mixture.
Continue stirring until comes back to a simmer, then stir briskly for 2 minutes.
Remove from heat, immediately fill 1 jar at a time to ¼" below the top. Wipe off top edge with clean damp paper towel. Secure lid and ring, and place upside down on a thick towel.
Continue with remaining jam, leaving 2" between jars.
After 5-7 minutes, carefully turn jars upright and leave undisturbed for 24 hours.
Check to be sure all jars have sealed, wipe clean and store in a cool, dark, dry place.
Although this is the method I have used for over 35 years with good success, the way to seal the jars that's recommended today is to process the filled jars in a hot water bath canner for 10 minutes before setting on the towel.

Options:
- Replace the honey with 2 cups raw sugar.
- Use 2 cups cooked quince mixture, 1 tsp calcium water, and ½ cup honey. Simmer on low for about 1 hour, stirring every few minutes until mixture thickens. (Hold a wooden spoon up from the jam and 2 drops should fall at the same time.) The jam will reduce down considerably. The flavor is quite different, and an old style quince will turn a beautiful reddish color. (There's always extra calcium powder, and it's fun to see the difference.)

Notes:
- Pomona Fruit Pectin brand is the source of the pectin powder and calcium powder.
- Each batch (when honey is used) produces 4-5 cups of jam.
- The whole 3 ¼# of quince produces 2 ½-3 batches.
- For other fruit jams, I recommend using the recipes that comes with the Pomona pectin.

A word of caution: Rhubarb jam won't set if more than 2 tsp calcium water is used.

Chickpea Hummus & More**

This is great cold with raw veggies, your favorite chips, or in a sandwich.

2 cups drained chickpeas
2 T tahini
4-6 T fresh lemon juice
1 large clove garlic, sliced thick (1T)
¼ tsp cumin
¾ tsp whole salt
2 T xv olive oil

Add all to a food processor. Blend 2-4 minutes until very smooth.
Store covered in fridge for up to 6 days.

Options:
- Double the garlic for super garlic hummus.
- Start with 4 T lemon juice. Add more to taste. Some like a bit more cumin also.

Other bean options:
- For pinto beans, black beans, or white beans: reduce lemon juice to 2 T, olive oil to 1 ½ T.
- For white bean humus, also double the cumin to ½ tsp.
- These three are also good as a warm dip.

Note: All 4 dips have even better flavor after chilling for 12-24 hours.

Olive Oil & Herb Dip*

This is a quick, satisfying snack you can take anywhere.

¼ cup xv olive oil
½ tsp dried basil
¼ tsp dried oregano
½ tsp garlic powder
¼ tsp whole salt
1 clove garlic, thinly sliced (optional)

Thick slices of whole grain bread cut into 1 ½" cubes.

Mix together all but bread.
Cover and let it rest on the counter for 1-10 hours, stirring occasionally.
Dip the bread in and enjoy.

This is a nice start to a pasta/salad meal, or mixed right into any pasta of your choice.

Almond Milk**

Great in hot or cold cereals, shakes, or as a refreshing nutritious drink.

2 cups water
3-5 pitted dates
⅓-½ cup soaked almonds*

Blend all in a Vitamix blender until liquefied.

Recommended: Use the higher amounts listed first, reducing the amount of almonds and dates until you find the ideal ratio for your taste buds, or specific recipe.

There will still be a few small particles left after blending, which need to be removed before using in all recipes except fruit shakes and drinks, as the mild grittiness will be apparent. The strained pieces can be added to hot cereals, breads, or muffins to name a few. (A nut milk bag for straining can be found at most natural foods stores, or sturdy cheese cloth will do.)

*Soaked almonds: Place ¾ cup almonds in a container, filling with water to at least 1" above nuts. Cover and store in fridge for 8-10 hours, or up to 2 days, replacing the water each day. Use freshly made milk within 24 hours. This recipe is geared toward shakes and drinks, but can replace soy milk in most recipes, although the texture and taste will be a little different.

Please note: If you need a large amount of almond milk and are short on time, unsweetened almond milk is available in stores. I have used it in rice pudding and soups, for example, and have been happy with the results. If replacing soy milk with almond milk, I recommend using no more than half the salt called for in the recipe.

Hot Chocolate**

Homemade hot chocolate and warm cookies produce long sighs and big smiles.

4 tsp raw sugar
2 ½ tsp unsweetened cocoa powder
¼ tsp vanilla powder
¹⁄₁₆ tsp xanthan gum powder
Couple grains of salt (optional)

Whisk all together, then whisk into a huge mug of hot plain soy milk or almond milk.

Hot Carob:
- Briskly whisk 2 ½ tsp roasted carob powder into a large hot mug of vanilla soy milk.
- Or equal parts of roasted carob powder can be substituted for cocoa powder in above recipe.

Peach Tea**

This is such a refreshing drink. The tea and juice flavors meld together well for a wonderful flavor with a hint of sweetness.

4 cups boiling water
3 black tea bags, regular or decaf (common orange pekoe tea is fine)
6 oz. of 100% white grape and peach juice frozen concentrate
2 ½ cups water

Place the tea bags in a large heat-proof container, such as a half gallon mason jar.
Pour in the boiling water and let it steep 30 minutes or more. (If you prefer to keep the steeping time under 5 minutes as is generally recommended, use 4 bags for 3-5 minutes.)
When cooled add juice and remaining water. Chill in fridge and enjoy.

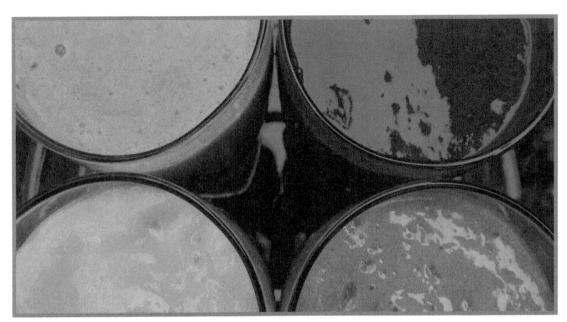

Breakfast

Breakfast Shakes**

The quickest, most refreshing breakfast, or lunch.
Good in the cooler weather, simply divine in the summer!

Protein shake:
1 batch fresh almond milk (2-3 cups)
1 T chia seeds
2 T almond butter
1 banana, peeled and frozen

Fruit shake:
1 batch fresh almond milk
1 T chia seeds
1 ½ cups frozen fruit

Blend in a Vitamix blender until smooth. Enjoy.

Shakes pictured: Mango with greens (kale), mango, strawberry, and blueberry.

Options for either shake:
- Replace almond milk with plain soy milk, adding 4-5 pitted dates.
- For extra sweetness, add 1 T honey.

Nice fruit combos:
- Strawberries, blueberries, raspberries, and blackberries (aka thimbleberries): 2, 3, or all 4 together.
- Peaches and blueberries
- Mango and young kale leaves (Pictured above. Worth making just for the color!)

Other good additions: Add ½ avocado, 2 T hemp seeds, 2 or 3 ice cubes, and/or a small handful of any fresh greens from the garden for the really adventurous.

Good Hot Oatmeal**

Why an oatmeal recipe? For anyone who has endured a bowl more closely resembling lumpy glue and hopes for better, this is your recipe.

1 ½ cups water
1 cup quick oats

Place the water in a small pan, cover and bring just to a boil.
Remove from the heat, quickly stir in the oats, cover and let sit for 5 minutes.
Pour into a bowl, add your favorite fresh fruit, sweetener, and a little almond milk or rice milk.
  Mmmm.
Enough for 1 very hungry person or two light eaters.

Option: Hot Quinoa - Bring 1 cup water and ½ cup white quinoa to a boil. Cover and simmer 15 minutes, add your favorite goodies as above and enjoy.

Mango Crème**

Mmm... fruity, creamy, and spicy!

1, 6-8 oz. container vanilla soy yogurt
1 large mango, peeled and pitted
½"-¾" fresh ginger, sliced (½-1 T)
1 T honey

Blend all in a Vitamix blender until smooth and creamy.
For a thicker drink, freeze prepared mango overnight.

Fruity Nutty Pancakes

2 ¼ - 2 ½ cups plain soy milk
1 tsp apple cider vinegar
¼ cup light olive oil
1 T maple syrup
1 tsp vanilla extract
1 cup finely ground old fashioned oats

⅓ cup spelt flour
⅓ cup kamut flour
1 tsp whole salt
⅓ cup oat bran
2 tsp baking powder
½ tsp baking soda

½-¾ cup chopped pecans or walnuts
1 ½ cups fresh blueberries, or any other diced fruit

Whisk together the first 6 ingredients in the order listed. Allow to rest for at least 10 minutes.
In a separate bowl mix together the next 6 ingredients.
Gradually stir the dry into the wet with the whisk until just moistened.
Fold in nuts and fruit of your choosing.
The batter should be thin enough to spread out on a hot griddle but thick enough to stop at a
    thickness of approx 3/16".
Preheat griddle on medium heat. Pour on griddle leaving at least 1" between.
Pancakes are ready to flip when bubbles have formed on top and a couple have popped.
If the pancakes are too dark when flipped, reduce heat a bit.
Remove when the bottoms are nicely browned. (As with all pancakes: if they are cooked too little,
    they will be gooey; too long, they will be dry and stiff.) Pour on the pure maple syrup and enjoy!

Maple Granola

This is great any time of day with rice milk or almond milk, not to mention on top of banana ice cream!

Preheat oven to 300 degrees

Dry ingredients:
12 cups (2 ¾#) old fashioned oats
2 cups oat bran
2 cups dry unsweetened coconut flakes
⅓ cup sesame seeds
1 ½ cups pecans, chopped
1 ½ cups sunflower seeds

Wet ingredients:
1 ½ cups pure maple syrup
2 tsp vanilla extract
1 tsp whole salt
¾ cup water
1 cup liquefied xv coconut oil, still warm

Mix together the 6 dry ingredients in a large roasting pan.
Mix the 5 wet ingredients together (shaken up in a quart mason jar works well) and stir very well into the dry. (It will be quite wet.)
Place half the mixture into the bottom of another large roasting pan.
Even out in both pans to approx 1 ½" deep.
Bake 300 degrees. Stir thoroughly (including scraping the bottom and leveling) after baking 20, 15, 12, 10, and 10 minutes. Remove from oven when golden brown (may take an additional 5-10 minutes).
Cool completely, and store in an air tight container to be used within a couple weeks, with the remainder into the freezer.

Options:
- Substitute 1 ¼ cups raw sugar for maple syrup, and increase water to 2 cups. The granola will harden as it cools. Using the raw sugar generally takes approx 10 minutes less.
- An equal amount of olive oil may be used in place of the coconut oil.

Muesli*

This raw cereal will give you the boost you're looking for.
Add rice milk (or your favorite grain beverage) for a delicious breakfast, lunch or a quick snack!

10-12 cups (2 ¾ #) old fashioned (regular) oats
½ cup oat bran*
½ cup brown unhulled sesame seeds
1 cup toasted wheat germ
1 cup dried unsweetened coconut flakes
¾ cup sliced almonds
1 cup raisins
½ cup walnuts chopped
½ cup pecans chopped
½ cup granulated 100% maple sugar
½ cup sunflower seeds
1 cup dates, chopped fine (approx 10 pitted)

Mix all ingredients together. (The dates may need to be mixed with 1-2 T oat flour to separate.)
Store in the freezer whatever won't be eaten in a week.

Options:
1. Replace maple sugar with raw sugar.
2. Gluten Free Option: In place of ½ cup oat bran and 1 cup toasted wheat germ, use 1 ½ cups of only toasted oat bran. For non-gluten free, you could use all toasted wheat germ. (Using raw in this recipe is not recommended.)
3. To 1 cup muesli, mix in ¾ cup lukewarm water. Cover and soak 18-24 hours in the fridge before eating. ¼ tsp fresh lemon juice may also be added for a little extra zip.
4. Replace 1 or 2 cups of regular oats with quick oats.

5. For more crunch in your muesli: Mix together all the following ingredients:

        ½ cup walnuts, chopped

        ½ cup pecans, chopped

        2 T unsweetened, dried coconut flakes

        ½ cup regular oats

        ¼ tsp vanilla

        1 tsp water

        1 tsp light olive oil or liquefied coconut oil

Spread onto a cookie sheet greased with coconut oil. Bake: 300 degrees for 7 minutes. Stir up and bake another 5-7 minutes until lightly browned. Cool completely and add to muesli.

*To toast oat bran: Preheat oven to 300 degrees. Spread out evenly on a cookie sheet with sides and bake 10-15 minutes, stirring up every 5 minutes. When slightly browned and fragrant, remove from oven and cool completely.

Tips Worth Reading

Tips Worth Reading

New information for some; good reminders for everyone!

- Trying healthier foods for the first time? Give yourself three months minimum of eating fresh, whole foods to develop taste buds that remember what good food tastes like that's not overloaded with sugar, salt, and fat. By then, the super sugary foods will seem too sweet and lacking in real flavor.

- Always read the entire recipe before starting, and double check amounts at the end.

- Be alert and focused while preparing food and working near hot surfaces to minimize burned or cut fingers.

ABBREVIATIONS: T=tablespoon, tsp=teaspoon (See p. 8 for complete list.)

BAKING:

- Ideally, bring all ingredients to room temperature by setting out 15-20 minutes ahead. One exception would be flour for pastry dough, which needs to be kept frozen until ready to use.

- "Cut in" means to push down with a pastry cutter at different angles to combine the ingredients to a fine crumble.

- When measuring baking powder or baking soda, push down to make sure it is packed in the measuring spoon, then level off, exerting some pressure as you go. Make sure any clumps are broken up before adding to your dry mix, by squishing it with a smaller spoon while adding it.

- Especially in baked goods, mixing the dry ingredients together well, and then separately mixing the wet ingredients well, and lastly just lightly and gradually mixing the dry into the wet until just moistened will produce a light, uniform product.

- Always preheat your oven which means to bring the temperature up to desired temp before adding food.

- To grease baking pans, use a thin layer of Earth Balance margarine. Oiling with coconut oil or olive oil is fine too, but some things may stick a bit.

- Make sure baked goods are of uniform size and thickness to ensure even cooking, with enough space left between to allow for expansion.

- Bake everything with the oven rack on the middle shelf unless specified otherwise.

- Steps to take if your baked goods are burning on the bottom before the tops are done: 1. Double check that the actual oven temp is accurate. 2. Raise oven rack up one notch. 3. The batter may need a bit more flour. If not firm enough, it will take too long for the center to set and the outside will get over cooked. 4. Bake a batch on a higher rack and reduce temp by 25 degrees.

- Let muffins and quick breads set in their baking tin for 10 minutes on a cooling rack before carefully removing.

BRANDS: Fruit thickener used to make jams was **Pomona fruit pectin.**

- **Molasses** used in recipes should be **Barbados** or unsulfured unless blackstrap is specifically mentioned.
- **Muir Glen pizza sauce** and **pasta sauce** were used when homemade was not available.
- Non hydrogenated margarine used in recipes was **Earth Balance** brand.
- Veggie **bouillon** used was **Rapunzel** brand veggie cubes with sea salt.
- Veggie ground used in recipes was **Yves** brand veggie ground.

BREAD: When making bread, remember to slowly and gradually mix ingredients in the same direction. When kneading, knead slowly and gently for light, tender bread. Rushing through will produce heavy bricks.

- Hard red wheat makes good traditional bread with a good flavor. Hard white wheat makes a lighter bread, but not as flavorful. A mixture of both is nice. Substituting 3-4 cups of any other flour will give you a nice variety also.
- Be sure the water used in yeast breads is lukewarm. (Drop a couple drops on the inside of your wrist, it should be warm but not hot.) Water that's too hot will kill the yeast and your bread won't rise; too cold and it won't work well.
- Common sense note: Use a fuzz-free towel or oiled plastic wrap to drape over rising bread.
- To find out if your bread has finished baking, tap on the bottom. The outside should be a high pitch, the center a low pitch, signifying the bread is cooked all the way through.
- **FRESH BREAD CRUMBS:** Put whole grain bread that's dried out a bit into food processor and process until fine crumbs. Store in freezer.
- **TOASTED BREAD CRUMBS:** Spread single layer on cookie sheet. Bake at 325 degrees for 5-10 minutes until lightly browned.

FLOUR: A combination of spelt and kamut are used in many recipes because a growing number of people do not tolerate the current hybridized wheats, but can still tolerate these (me being one of them). In the future I plan to work on more gluten free recipes.

- Hard white wheat flour (100% whole grain) can be substituted for any combination of spelt or spelt/kamut in a recipe, but hold back some of the flour until the end of the mixing for proper consistency.

- If you plan on using whole grain flours in any appreciable amount, consider investing in a grain mill. We have mouse-impermeable garbage cans just for storing grain in our cool, dry basement. Any extra that is ground is kept in the freezer. Once you've used fresh ground flour, you'll never go back!

- When measuring flour, fluff up first, then fill your cup from a scoop and level off with a straight edge. (Chopsticks work nicely.) If the flour is clumpy (such as chickpea flour can be), sift first with a flour sifter, or place in a fine mesh strainer and work through with a spoon.

- When a recipe calls for flour, always reserve at least ½ cup of just flour to mix last as needed, as flours can have different densities and moisture content. If substituting flours, reserve more.

FREEZING: Many of the recipes are in large enough amounts for you to also freeze some for ready-made meals another day.

- To keep food in the freezer longer, be sure to remove air pockets before sealing freezer bags, and leaving only enough space at the top in containers to allow for expansion as the food freezes (¼"- ½") depending on how much water the food contains. FYI, if you use a glass container and don't leave enough space it may break.

FRYING: When heating a frying pan on the stove top, if you use a flame stovetop, set the heat where you want it, and wait approximately 4 minutes for it to reach that temperature. Turning it on high to speed it up and then turning it down does not produce the same results.

GARLIC: Organic, homegrown, hard neck garlic is used in the recipes. One 'toe' or clove of this garlic produces approximately 1 T of minced or chopped garlic. Other kinds may need more than one clove. My secret for large cloves of garlic? Find a local source of untreated garlic bulbs. Split into single cloves saving only the outside cloves to plant. Idealy, plant in loamy, well drained soil. Plant 4" down, 6" apart, 10" between the rows and cover with 4"-5" of mulch. In the northeast, I plant the first couple weeks in October and dig it up the first or second week in July. Dig one up and check: if the cloves are well formed and the tops have partially died back, it is ready. If the outside sheaths on the bulb are peeling away (or rotting off) the bulb, you waited too long; dig them up quick! Take care in digging and handling, as fresh garlic is more easily damaged. Immediately hang each separate piece in a dry area out of direct sunlight with constant air flow. We have designated two-by-fours to staple gun the stalks to, then suspend the boards from a couple loops from the ceiling in the garage. (Leave a good foot or so on the ends so there isn't a chance of them slipping off the loops and falling.) Then store them in staggered bunches in the cool, dry, dark basement around October. If you have a root cellar, even better. Remember to plant the best and eat the rest for bigger and better garlic each year.

GARLIC GRANULES are recommended over garlic powder, as the powder has a tendency to clump over time.

HERBS used in recipes refer to dried herbs unless it specifies fresh. (The general rule of thumb is: You can substitute 1T fresh chopped herbs for 1 tsp dried.)

HONEY: Use local honey if at all possible. It will contain the pollens from your own surroundings which some people find beneficial, and the taste by far surpasses store-bought honey. Also consider this; the store-bought honey generally does not show which countries the honey comes from or those countries' allowances regarding pesticides.

LECITHIN: Why lecithin in some recipes? It works as an emulsifier in recipes such as soups and sauces. It holds 100% whole grain breads together better as well as keeping them fresh longer, and it is a good nutrient to be consuming anyway!

LEGUMES: All cooked beans used in recipes were fresh cooked from dried beans. If you use canned beans, be sure to rinse to remove some of the salt, or use ones that contain only beans and water.

- Always sort dried beans and lentils before rinsing and using. Look for small stones, clumps of soil, and any odd or damaged beans.

- Use the most recent crop of dried beans when possible. Beans that are several years old take longer to cook, and generally don't taste as good.

LEMON JUICE: Always use fresh squeezed lemon juice for superior flavor.

MILKS: Rice milk used was Rice Dream original, enriched.

- Silk brand, unsweetened almond milk may be substituted for soy milk in any recipe.

- Soy milk used in recipes was Silk brand, original flavor found in the refrigerated section.

OILS: Remember, good fats/oils not only add flavor and texture to our foods, they are essential to our bodies working properly.

- **Oil abbreviations:** xv = extra virgin, xvoo = extra virgin olive oil, xvco = extra virgin coconut oil. In some cookbooks, you might also see, "ev" for extra virgin or "evoo" for extra virgin olive oil. The abbreviation "xv" was common for a while, then "ev" became the popular one.

- **Oil heat levels:** Xvco, xvoo, or light olive oil are interchangeable in the recipes with the exception of frying. If frying at a higher temp, xvco, peanut oil, or sesame oil will smoke less then light olive oil, with xvoo most susceptible to smoking. It sets off the smoke alarm pretty quickly too. (Smoking, burning oil needs to be thrown out.) Xvco will quickly liquefy on low heat to then be used in recipes. If trying to transition from light olive oil to xvoo in some recipes, fruity xvoo is good to use to help you adjust to the stronger flavor. The different oils will of course produce a slightly different taste, so have fun experimenting to find your personal favorite!

- Another great use for **xv coconut oil**: Squish ½-1 T through your teeth for 15-20 minutes to freshen your breath (with or without 2-4 drops of oregano oil mixed with it). Spit out oil, then rinse mouth with warm water and spit out, along with all the junk the oil just pulled out.

ONIONS: Before using, remove the 1-3 outer skins, down to the more tender layers. Red or white sweet onions were used in all salad recipes. Either white sweet or yellow cooking onions are used in the rest, unless scallions are specified. The sweet will produce a milder onion flavor if you prefer, and the yellow a more pronounced flavor. (The outer layers are fine for vegetable stock.)

ORGANIC: Start with fresh, organic ingredients whenever possible. How good your food tastes, first and foremost, depends on the ingredients that go in.

OTHER COOKBOOKS: Should you want to take the next step in super healthy recipes, I recommend checking out the recipe books by Rhonda Malkmus, which coincide with the Hallelujah Diet based on Genesis 1:29.

PANS: Save yourself years of frustration—invest in thick bottom pans for even heating and to reduce the risk of burning. Cast iron is my favorite. Read the label carefully for care instructions.

PARSLEY: Fresh Italian flat leaf parsley is recommended in all recipes. It makes a nice breath freshening snack also!

PEANUT BUTTER used is natural, 100% peanut butter with no additives, just peanuts. Mix well before measuring.

PIE CRUST ROLLING INSTRUCTIONS: Use a cloth-covered rolling pin to roll out pie dough. First flatten the dough out with floured hands to approx ⅜" thick and relatively circular. Slowly roll out on a floured pastry cloth with even pressure. To create a round disk, think of a clock. Starting at the center each time, roll to 12 o'clock, then 6; to 3 then 9; to 2 then 8; to 10 then 4. Then start again until desired thickness. (About ⅛" thick.) Fold dough and cloth in half once rolled out. Remove the cloth as you slide the dough halfway over pie plate then carefully unfold. Gently situate dough to touch all sides and base. Add filling. (Cut overhanging dough to 1" for single crust, shorter for double crust, leaving top crust with 1" overhang.) Fold top crust under bottom crust, and pinch together in your own decorative style. Roll out any excess dough again, cut into 2" squares, sprinkle with a 1:4 cinnamon/sugar ratio, if you like, and bake 4-5 minutes at 400 until crisp and lightly browned. Gives everyone something to snack on while the pie bakes!

POTATOES: Before using, always rinse and scrub well, removing eyes (sprout spots) and bad spots. The nice looking part of the skins may be left. I prefer russet potatoes in most recipes, and Yukon Golds are nice. Every kind has a slightly different taste and texture. Try a variety of potatoes to discover your own favorites.

OATS: Quick oats = quick oats, not instant oats. **Reg oats** = regular, old fashioned oats

SALAD: To assure veggies stay crisp, make sure the grains are completely cool before adding remaining ingredients in salads.

SALT: Using solely a whole salt is strongly recommended, as it contains approx 50-80 minerals our bodies need in a more absorbable form, as opposed to just NaCl in the highly refined table salt. Two kinds are Himalaya Salt, and Real Salt brand. Use in common sense moderation. An interesting experiment: remove all refined salt from your diet for the day, prepare your meals with whole salt, then see how thirsty you are afterwards. Another day use refined table salt in the same quantity in your meal and see how thirsty you are afterwards. Most will be much less thirsty with the whole salt because your body is absorbing the minerals in it, as opposed to trying to flush out the refined table salt from your system. You be the judge.

SEEDS, NUTS, AND GRAINS: Use raw unless otherwise stated.

- **CHIA SEEDS:** Be sure to soak first, as they absorb a large amount of water. Shake up in a container 1 T seeds with ⅔ cup water. Refrigerate overnight. Use within 2 days. You can add soaked chia seeds to, well, pretty much anything you want! Keep the heat used in the recipe to under 350 degrees. Try original recipes first before adding chia seeds.

- **GRINDING FLAX SEEDS AND SESAME SEEDS:** Freeze at least overnight before grinding to keep the seeds from getting too warm when grinding. (Do not use flax seeds that are ground at a high temp.) Place ⅔-¾ cup seeds in Vitamix. Grind 10-15 seconds on high. Remove from base, stir up and repeat until finely ground. Do gradually or you will end up with seed butter instead. Keep extra ground seeds in the freezer. Fresh ground flax seeds should have a clean, fresh scent; if you buy some already ground that do not, take them back to the store. If you're not interested in a few extra crunchies in your food, sift the fresh ground seeds through a medium-fine sieve to catch the few that did not grind up completely. Don't want to waste them? Toss them in your next shake.

- **SESAME SEEDS:** Brown, unhulled sesame seeds are mostly tan and cream colored. They are so much better in the recipes than the white hulled ones whose nutritious little coats (hulls) have been removed!

- **WHITE QUINOA GRAIN** is used unless otherwise specified.

SOUPS: Interested in making the cream soups gluten free? Omit the flour, bring the completed soup to a simmer, measure out half as much arrowroot powder to the amount of flour called for (e.g., for ½ cup flour, use ¼ cup arrowroot), shake that up with enough water to liquefy, then pour into the simmering soup, stirring until it thickens. If you prefer a thicker soup, gradually stir in more arrowroot/water mixer, bringing the soup back to a simmer after each addition.

- Most soups, and mashed potatoes, will absorb moisture overnight. When warming them back up, mix in a small amount of the original liquid (e.g., soy milk or water), keeping in mind the food will thin out some when warmed up.

STORING: A **general rule** of thumb: the more nutritious, the more perishable. For example, whole grain flour should be kept in the freezer so the nutritious wheat germ in it doesn't go rancid. That white flour sitting in the cupboard that hasn't spoiled weeks if not months later has little to no food value.

- Keep **all food tightly covered** once completely cooled, whether left on counter (such as cookies), in fridge or freezer.

- Keep your **fridge** at 35 degrees with space in between containers to discourage freezing or warmer spots to develop. Place a fridge thermometer in varying levels, front and back overnight. Check temp in morning. While you're at it, put one in the freezer too. Keeping food frozen to 0 degrees is helpful.

- Store **dried herbs** in a cool, dark place. Using within a year would be best. After two years, toss them in the compost bin.

- Placing dried bay leaves in with **stored grains and beans** helps to keep away the weevils, moths, and larvae that can be a problem, especially in warm weather. (Your flour is in the freezer, of course.) For example, put two leaves in a 4-5 pound container of old fashioned oats; put 3-4 oz of leaves in the bottom of the can the bag of grain is stored in, adding another 4 oz once a year.

STOVE: Experiment with your stovetop so you know the actual location of settings for low, medium and high. With electric, boil water to barely a simmer, then a medium boil, then a rolling boil, and see where the gauge is set then. With a gas stove, visually look at the flame then see where the gauge is. The accuracy of the controls can vary considerably from stove to stove.

- Invest in an **oven thermometer** and check actual temp at varying degrees before getting started. For example, 250, 350, and 450.

- **NEVER LEAVE A STOVE ON UNATTENDED!**

- Use a **timer.** We all can get distracted easily and time passes quicker than we realize. Look for a very loud obnoxious one, for the same reason!

SUGAR Raw sugar can replace maple sugar in any recipe.

TOFU: Regular tofu is used in the recipes, not the silken style.

VANILLA = vanilla extract

VEGGIES: All **cooked** veggies are better when only cooked to **crisp-tender.** That especially applies to cauliflower, broccoli, and asparagus; their flavor completely changes when over cooked, and not for the better.

- **CRISP-TENDER** means the vegetables are cooked until they are still slightly crisp when bit into, but taste cooked not raw.

- Not crazy about cooked veggies? Great! Eat plenty of them **raw** by themselves or drag them through your favorite bean dip for a quick lunch.

VITAMIX brand is the blender used in these recipes. An average blender is not powerful enough. Blend most things in Vitamix on high, adding liquid first. Be sure the lid is secure!

YAMS VS SWEET POTATOES: My Mom always called them sweet potatoes, but we always bought yams. Try both, see which you prefer. For a nutritious snack, bake any kind of potato at 375 degrees for approximately 1 hour (turning and pricking with a fork after 30 minutes). Slice in two, drizzle with xv olive oil, a sprinkle of garlic powder, whole salt and enjoy! When baking "sweet potatoes," place on an oiled piece of aluminum foil on a cookie sheet to catch the sticky drips.

YEAST: Active dry yeast was used in the recipes. Store in an airtight container in the fridge for up to a year, or store part of it in the freezer for several years. 1-2 pound vacuum-packed containers are much more reasonably priced than the 1T packets found in grocery stores.

CPSIA information can be obtained at www.ICGtesting.com
Printed in the USA
BVOW11s0103291113

337583BV00002B/2/P

9 780985 524173